# THE BOOK OF SOBA

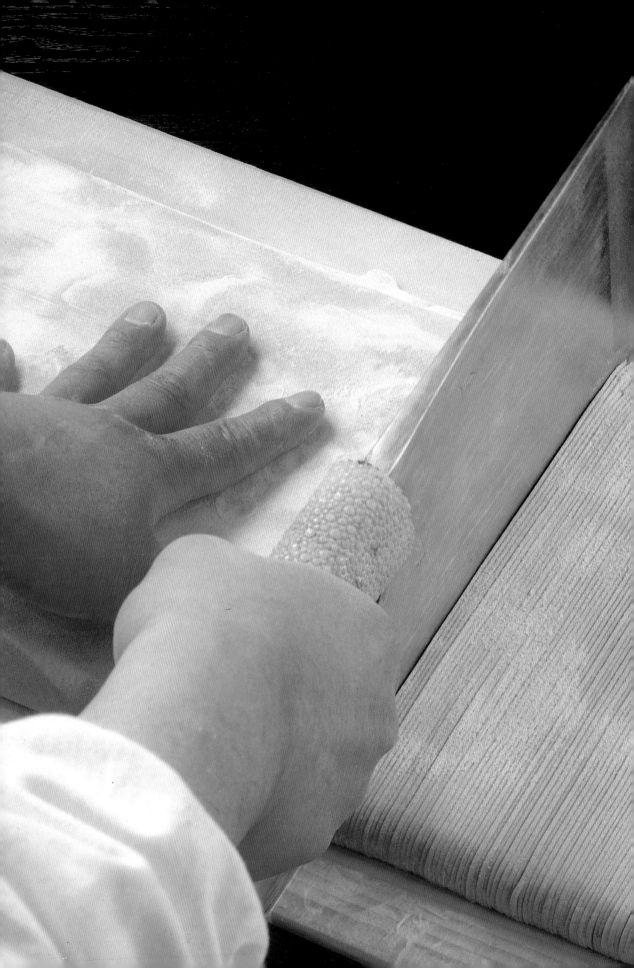

# THE BOOK OF
# SOBA

## JAMES UDESKY

with a foreword by
## WILLIAM SHURTLEFF

KODANSHA INTERNATIONAL
Tokyo and New York

*To Grandmother Haus, 97, whose strong constitution and love of nature nurtured me in my youth, and to my mother and father, whose continual patience and assistance allowed me to see this project through to completion.*

641.822
UDE

Half-title page: Flavored Soba Noodles

Distributed in the United States by Kodansha International/ USA Ltd., through Harper & Row, Publishers, Inc., 10 East 53rd Street, New York, New York 10022.

Published by Kodansha International Ltd., 2-2, Otowa 1-chome, Bunkyo-ku, Tokyo 112 and Kodansha International/ USA Ltd., 10 East 53rd Street, New York, New York 10022.

First printing, 1988

**Library of Congress Cataloging-in-Publication Data**
Udesky, James, 1951–
　The book of soba.
　Bibliography: p.
　Includes index.
　1. Cookery (Buckwheat) 2. Soba (Noodles)
　3. Cookery, Japanese. I. Title.
TX809.B8U28　　1988　　641.8'22　　87-82855

ISBN 0-87011-860-9 (U.S.)
ISBN 4-7700-1360-4 (Japan)

# CONTENTS

# Foreword

It is a great honor and pleasure for me to write the foreword to *The Book of Soba*. Since my friend James Udesky outlined his long-term project to me some years ago, I have followed its progress with great interest. Now his efforts have borne fruit, and the result is an important and original contribution.

Although the Japanese word "soba" also refers to the buckwheat plant and its seeds, I will use it here to refer only to buckwheat noodles, which are one of Japan's most important traditional foods. Soba is a food both democratic and elite, distinguished by being indispensable in both Japan's popular food culture and in its classic haute cuisine. To understand soba is to understand the heart of Japanese food culture. Indeed the world of soba in Japan is a microcosm of the best of all Japanese culture.

My wife Akiko and I lived in Japan for seven years (1971–77) studying foods, and especially soy foods such as tofu, miso, soy sauce, and *natto*. For us the word "soba" brings back a host of good memories: at Kyoto's Izumo Soba we watched the craftsman make handmade soba in the shop's front window. He rolled out the dough into a huge, thin round using a slender, yard-long wooden rolling pin, then folded it serpentine-fashion, and deftly sliced it crosswise with an elegant five-inch-tall soba knife into tender, fresh noodles. Here, I thought, was the Japanese counterpart of Italy's tosser of fresh pizza rounds. My favorite at Izumo was Soba Noodles with Whipped Mountain Yam, the freshly grated yam atop the soba in a steaming hot broth. This type of hot soba was exquisite on cold winter nights! In inexpensive but cozy restaurants we enjoyed noodles and tempura served on a graceful little tray of thin bamboo strips and accompanied by a separate cup of dipping sauce. I still have visions of the young man from the local soba shop racing on his bicycle with an order for home delivery balanced precariously on one hand above his head. Twice we traveled to the Nagano-Shinshu area, the center of buckwheat growing and processing in Japan. And each New Year's Eve, like all Japanese, we downed *Toshikoshi Soba*, which carries its own wish for a long life in the new year and years ahead.

To enjoy and study soba at its elegant best, we visited Yabu Soba in Kanda, Tokyo. We immediately sensed that this famous generations-old soba shop was special—the home of an almost timeless, pure Japanese form: the elegant yet simple decor, the beautiful utensils and fabrics, the presence of nature, the warm and attentive service, and the satisfying, light food.

We are not the first generation of Westerners to take a deep interest in Japanese foods. The first were those European travelers who managed to enter isolated Japan during the 1600s and 1700s. From men like Captain John Saris (1613), Englebert Kaempfer (1712), Per Osbeck (1771), and Karl Peter Thunberg (1784), we get our first sketches of a world of food and drink vastly different from our own. Kaempfer traveled in Japan from 1690 to 1692. In his classic *Amoenitatum Exoticarum*, published in Latin in Germany in 1712, he gave the Chinese character for buckwheat, then wrote, "Kjo [pronounced Kyo], vulgo Soba, Fagopyrum sativum. Frumentum Sarasenicum." He made no mention of buckwheat noodles.

The second wave arrived in the 1880s, after Commodore Matthew Perry forced Japan to open its doors to Western influence. The emperor Meiji imported a host of top European professors to staff his new universities, and many of them wrote extensively about Japanese foods, often in great detail.

The third wave of interest arose some ninety years later, following World War II, and many of these traveler-students had their roots in the American and European natural-food and macrobiotic movements. Many learned Japanese, focused on the study of a small group of important foods, and wrote. Equally important, they generally worked to export to their native countries the foods they were studying. By the late 1970s and early 1980s large amounts of traditional Japanese foods were being imported by the Western world and enjoyed by a new health-conscious generation.

Akiko and I are part of this most recent wave, as is James Udesky. We first had the pleasure of meeting James in January 1976 in San Francisco. He was studying with Noboru Muramoto, a Japanese teacher of macrobiotics, and was deeply interested in *mochi*, herbs, and miso. We met again in Japan later that year—James had come to buy *mochi* machines. I encouraged him to pursue his interest in studying Japanese foods and shared with him some of my methods for doing research, writing, and learning Japanese. We met and talked numerous times during the following years and I was delighted to see that he decided to do it the right way: to become an apprentice of a true soba master and to take the time to go deep and learn the old ways.

Buckwheat has been cultivated in Japan for over 1,100 years, and soba (buckwheat noodles) has been made for more than 300 years. While studying soyfoods in Japan, I observed that behind every classical Japanese food is both an ancient tradition and a time-honored craft. For masters of this craft, it is a deep daily practice, for some even a spiritual practice, that nourishes both the craftsman and those who partake of his food. James Udesky is the first Westerner to become a soba master.

Thus, this book is a rich source of original information, based on a three-year apprenticeship, careful study and translation of Japanese documents on soba, and extensive contacts with experts in the field. Another rich realm of Japanese food culture has been transmitted to the West. And the timing is excellent, for there is currently a revival of interest in buckwheat and soba in America and the world.

During the late 1960s and the 1970s in America and Europe, natural food and macrobiotic companies (such as Chico-San, Erewhon, Westbrae, Eden, and Lima) began to import soba and publicize its many virtues. Although most Japanese soba presently contains 20 to 40 percent buckwheat flour (the rest is wheat flour), these companies reintroduced the traditional type containing 80 percent or more buckwheat flour. Many natural-food stores now also sell buckwheat groats and flour.

In addition, during the 1980s, nutritionists have come to recognize the importance of whole grains and complex carbohydrates in Western diets that are so overloaded with saturated fats and cholesterol (largely from meat) that large numbers of adults die of heart disease. In the world's three great pasta countries (China, Japan, and Italy), where grains are still a major part of the diet, rates of heart disease are low. Happily, in America pasta has now risen to the status of an "in" food.

Finally, agronomists are realizing that buckwheat—a plant which grows well in poor, dry, marginal soil, even in northern latitudes with short growing seasons—provides solid nutrition and can play a key role in feeding more and more people on less and less land. Here is an under-utilized plant whose time has come.

What Johnny Appleseed did for apples, James Udesky is doing for buckwheat and for soba. May he be equally successful!

WILLIAM SHURTLEFF

# Introduction

Among the main foods featured in traditional Japanese cuisine, sushi, tofu, and miso are now receiving increasing attention around the world. People concerned with their weight, cholesterol level, and blood pressure, for example, are looking to the "wisdom of the East" for clues on how to solve these problems from a dietary point of view.

At the same time that these foods are becoming accepted, soba cuisine (buckwheat noodles), a veritable giant within the world of traditional Japanese foods, is just now beginning to receive its due share of notice and appreciation in the West.

Having had a seven year background in the natural foods previous to going to Japan, I was well prepared to discover, explore, and learn the secrets of yet another long-standing style of Japanese original cuisine. Although I had eaten and grown accustomed to the natural sweetness of such grains as brown rice, wheat, and corn, I had never realized that buckwheat and noodles made from freshly hulled and still-moist buckwheat flour could produce such a refreshing and sweet taste. Not, that is, until I had a chance invitation to go to a soba restaurant which serves handmade noodles from freshly ground flour.

Soba cuisine has enjoyed widespread popularity for over 400 years in Japan. One of the main reasons for its continued popularity is that its light, sweet taste, together with its substantial, energy-giving kilocalories, make soba a perfect food for any season. During the hot summer months when the heat drains your energy and appetite, a light snappy tray of cool soba noodles served with freshly grated horseradish and a chilled, but well-balanced dipping sauce constitutes a meal that revitalizes you and actually helps to stimulate your appetite. On the other hand during the cold winter months when you need a food to provide warmth and energy, Tempura Soba, Curry Soba, or other soba dishes served in a hot broth settle you down and hit the spot.

The word *soba* refers to "long and thin brownish noodles" served plain or in soup. It is also the Japanese word for buckwheat, the plant and even the whole kernel or groat itself. Often thought of as a grain, botanically speaking buckwheat is classified outside the family of staple grains (Gramineae) which includes wheat, rice, barley, rye, and oats among others. (See About Soba.) Because of its ability to grow from seed to mature kernel in only 75 days and to grow in even barren soil, historically, buckwheat has been of vital importance in times of famine. However, in an ideal environment, such as Nagano Prefecture in Japan, where it is often foggy, the temperatures rarely exceed 68°F even during the summer, and there is enough wind and insect-life for cross-pollination, the buckwheat will produce soba so sweet that it seems to have sugar mixed in. Of course there is none.

From the time that the buckwheat plant produces its first flower in the field until the time the long, thin, and sweet noodles are delicately placed on top of a finely lacquered tray, buckwheat goes through a "beating" like no other noodle. The name given to this process, te-uchi, literally means "beating the buckwheat dough by hand."

Quite different from spaghetti, ramen, udon, and other noodles made from wheat flour, buckwheat flour will not stretch easily. In fact, when making buckwheat noodles from 90 to 100 percent buckwheat flour (a technique called kiko-uchi or "pure soba"), you can hear the sound of the rolling pin being pushed into the dough and against the rolling board in quite a forceful and commanding way. You can tell without looking that the buckwheat dough is indeed going through a beating.

Keeping pace with soba's long history, the market for soba has grown considerably. In addition to the 6,000-plus factories making soba noodles on a large scale, there are over 40,000 shops which serve buckwheat noodles to the public. Of these 40,000, approximately 7,000 shops are in Tokyo. Breaking this figure down further, it would not be far off to estimate that out of these 7,000 shops less than 10 percent claim to offer handmade soba noodles. Still, of these 700, it is safe to say that only about 100 to 150 of these shops at most, really perform the entire process by hand.

The previous breakdown is necessary because it must be clearly understood from the beginning that all soba noodles are not the same. The places I visited and was apprenticed to fall into the last category. Within this world of soba, one finds masters spicier than their trusty wasabi. This is especially true of my first teacher Takeo Abe, owner of the Take Yabu restaurant in Kashiwa, near Tokyo. On entering his shop, you are seated on a raised tatami platform and handed the menu by the owner himself. On my first visit, my companion and I ordered one cool dish and one hot one apiece. Like any great artist, Abe watched us closely as the first order of Natto Soba was delivered. This dish featured freshly rolled and cut noodles, topped with fragrantly fermented soybeans (natto), seasoned with a pinch of ground sesame seeds. Alongside were thin, delicate shavings of bonito, crispy flakes of nori seaweed, razor-thin slices of scallion-type onions, and a deep orange colored egg yolk crowning the center. Accompanying this colorful arrangement was the Soba master's famed dipping sauce. Served chilled, it has a sophisticatedly rich and hearty taste. Mixing the ingredients together, we glanced at each other with apprehension. Soon we were both smiling. Here was food that was as refreshing and light as a salad, yet sweet and energy giving. The firm, light, and slippery texture of the noodles provided a distinctly clean feeling, with a sweet aftertaste. Yet above all, it was the balance between the wholesome buckwheat, the sensual "baconlike" fragrance of the broth, and the combination and variety of ingredients which was so appealing.

This balance was not there by chance. The dipping sauce, for example, used high-quality bonito stock (boiled 45 minutes), and then combined it with just the right amount of carefully selected soy sauce, *mirin* (Japanese cooking sherry), and sugar to complement the soba. Once blended the dipping sauce is allowed to sit for three days, as it mellows like wine, saké, soy sauce and miso.

Right then and there, as the master was clearing our dishes, I declared to him that I must learn how to make this kind of food. He responded enthusiastically, and said that he would give me the opportunity to learn everything. This meant not merely how to make the noodles and the soup, but, more importantly, to understand how to create the proper mood to enable the customer to appreciate this cuisine. It also included a commitment to an apprenticeship, which required daily practice sessions until the body could move with precision, quickness, and rhythm. The feeling for this rhythm, as well as the mental and physical stamina, cannot be acquired overnight.

I agreed to a six-month trial period, and ended up continuing my actual training for 3 years, at a total of three shops. During this period, I collected books and magazines, newspaper articles, and anything I could get my hands on, to learn more about the tradition, nutrition, and history of soba. Occasionally, I happened upon articles on the buckwheat situation around the world and I was able to catch a glimpse of buckwheat's long history in Europe, Asia, and America. Obviously, what had so fascinated me was nothing less than a giant of a food, steeped in close to four centuries of tradition.

Today, modern science is shedding new light on the verifiable, nutritional value of traditional foods and the important role they can play as part of our daily diet. Added to the recent resurgence in a high-fiber, low-fat pasta diet, soba provides a gourmet touch to pasta cuisine.

Having the opportunity to study with and observe some of the most earnest practitioners in the field, while living in the country where buckwheat cuisine has held an undeniable appeal to people of all ages, kindled an irrepressible desire to successfully communicate and reveal the wonder of fresh buckwheat, and the noodles which are produced from its flour. Hopefully, this book will, in like fashion, kindle other people's curiosity, and help them to discover and partake of this potentially invaluable nutritional food source.

# I

## MAKING
## SOBA

# Homemade Soba Noodles

Making soba noodles at home can be fun, creative, and, once you get the hang of it, rather an easy thing to do. By using the utensils and space available in the average kitchen, and by obtaining the freshest buckwheat flour available, you can make fresh buckwheat noodles that will delight, satisfy, and pleasantly surprise your family, friends, and guests.

The process will be described in an easy-to-follow, step-by-step method. In the beginning, let this serve as a guide. Later, use it as a springboard to develop your own methods. With each batch, try to improve your technique, speed, and sense of rhythm. After several attempts, you will gain a measure of confidence, and from then on you'll find yourself looking for occasions to whip up a fresh batch of noodles for an impromptu lunch or dinner party.

Keep in mind that if you can obtain fresh and sufficiently sifted flour, and then secondly perform the initial mixing of the water into the flour in such a way as to allow the buckwheat to develop its own viscosity, you are providing the two most important elements for making successful soba noodles.

INGREDIENTS

    *5¼ cups buckwheat flour\**

    *2¼ cups wheat flour*

     *2 cups water*

EQUIPMENT

    *Cutting board*

    *Rolling pin*

    *Broad, well-sharpened kitchen knife*

    *Plastic wrap*

    *Mixing bowl, large*

    *Strainer*

*For the beginner, a ratio of 3 parts wheat flour to 7 parts buckwheat flour is recommended. You might even have to settle for a 4 to 6 ratio if the flour is not so fresh and hence lacks binding power. By utilizing more wheat, you are able to take advantage of its gluten to help the flour bind together. As you become more adept and gain more confidence try a 2–8 variation.

Another trick of the trade to increase the binding power of the flour is to use boiling water in the initial mixing stages (about 80 percent of the total water used). This compensates for the absence of gluten in buckwheat flour. The boiling water quickly penetrates buckwheat's superior starch components as well as activates the binding power of its water-soluble proteins.

When using cold water, there are many other common variations used to supplement the binding power of the buckwheat. One is to beat an egg or two into the cold water before mixing it into the flour, while another is to mix grated mountain yam (*yama imo*) into the flour before adding the water. Other traditional methods in Japan include adding powdered burdock leaves, used for their elasticity, and soaked and mashed soybeans (see Soy-Soba Noodles). Experiment and develop your own "special blend" of preferred ingredients.

STEP 1

Combine the buckwheat and wheat flour in the mixing bowl. While mixing the flour together in a circular motion, add the water.

Rather than pouring it in all at once, add it little by little. At the same time, it is important to work quickly, adding 90 percent of the water within the first 30 to 45 seconds. The aim is to avoid forming any large clumps.

Using both hands, mix the moistened and unmoistened flour together. Don't worry about the binding of the flour together at this stage.

## Step 2

Using the palms and fingertips of both hands, quickly and rhythmically toss and press the flour between your hands. Let the flour pass through your fingers and fall back into the bowl. Repeat until all of the flour feels evenly moistened and starts to form small "pebbles."

## Step 3

Follow the three-part sequence below:

A: Grab some flour with each hand and close your fingers around it to squeeze.

B: Open your hand. You should find that the mixture has developed some viscosity.

C: Break this clump apart with your fingers and allow the bigger pebbles of dough to fall back into the bowl. Repeat this sequence 20 to 30 times (over a 2-minute period) with the remaining flour.

(The purpose of repeating these quick hand movements is to help the flour develop viscosity. As mysterious as it is strong, buckwheat's viscosity takes some coaxing. In scientific parlance this is referred to as "tapping" the binding powers of the water-soluble proteins. Professional soba makers refer to the stage when the viscosity becomes apparent as the "blossoming" of the dough. That is, the individual grains of flour have bound together and "blossomed" into pebble-sized clumps. In essence, in the first three steps you are taking pains to bring about the blossoming and to "build-up" a dough that is not just sticky, but one which will be firm, compact, binding, and smooth throughout. If your dough meets these four conditions, you can confidently expect to make a firm and elastic noodle.)

## STEP 4
Now that the base has been established, add the remaining water and repeat step 3 for 1 minute to mix. The pebbles will expand. The flour's viscosity is gradually "sprouting," causing it to bind together in increasingly larger pebbles.

## STEP 5

Next, these must be kneaded together to form one large ball of dough. Lean over and push down on the dough with extended arms, using the force of your back and shoulders (especially that of the shoulder-blade area). Knead the dough with a pumping motion, left-right-left-right, for 1 to 2 minutes.

Pack the dough together. Knead the portion of dough closest to you 5 to 10 times, rotate 90°, and knead again. Rotate and knead until the dough is smooth throughout.

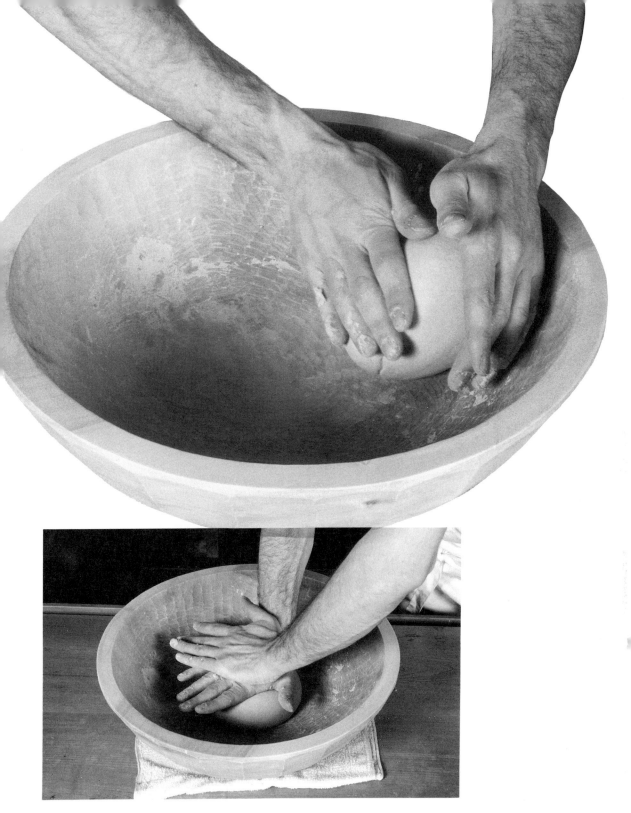

## STEP 6
Roll the dough around the inside of the edge of the bowl to prevent air pockets from forming, then flatten.

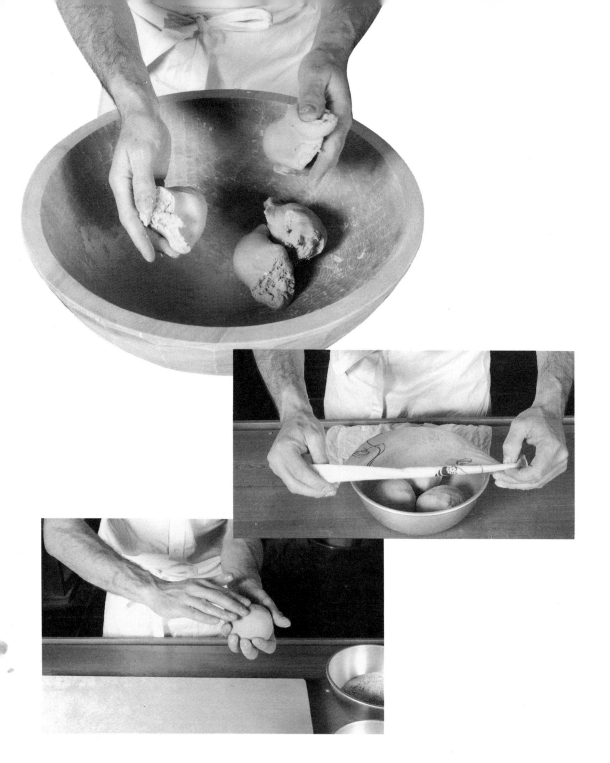

## STEP 7

Break the dough into 5 or 6 little balls and place them in another bowl. Cover with a damp cloth to prevent the dough from drying out (it dries quickly). Working with 1 ball at a time, roll it between your hands to smooth "from inside to out." Though sticky in the beginning, as you continue kneading it, it will become smooth and polished. When the dough is firm, roll it into a ball.

## STEP 8

Spread a little buckwheat flour over the surface of the cutting board and place a single, well-kneaded ball on top. Sprinkle with a little flour. Press down to flatten, then rotate and press to form a flat disc of dough.

With the rolling pin, roll out into an oval with a thickness of approximately ⅛ inch. The length should be about twice the width. Sprinkle with buckwheat flour as necessary to prevent sticking.

Sprinkle buckwheat flour on a piece of plastic wrap, lay the rolled-out dough on the plastic, and wrap it up. Repeat with the remaining balls of dough, placing each new flattened oval on top of the previous one. Sprinkle flour between each layer to prevent sticking.

1

2

3

4

5

6

STEP 9

When all the balls have been rolled out, return the stacked layers to the cutting board. Cut the layers in half and stack neatly, cut ends aligned. Fold in half.

To cut, place the left palm on the dough and "shave" off ⅛-inch-wide noodles with the knife, moving it forward and through the dough.

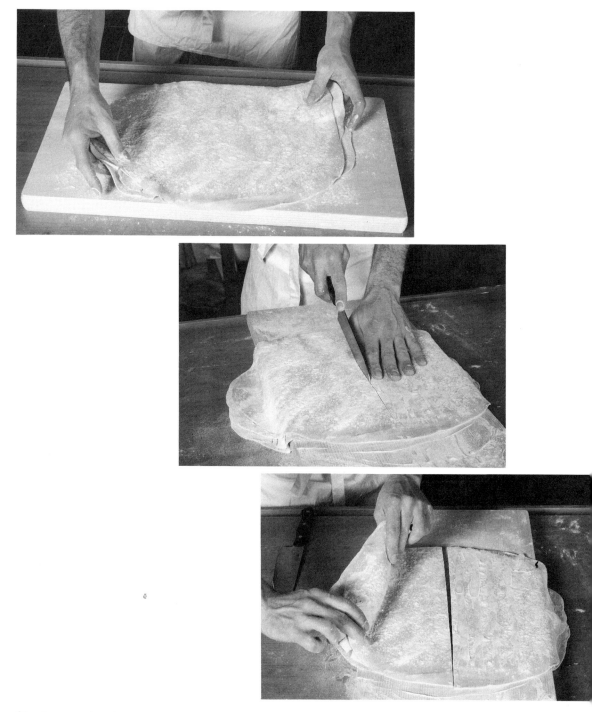

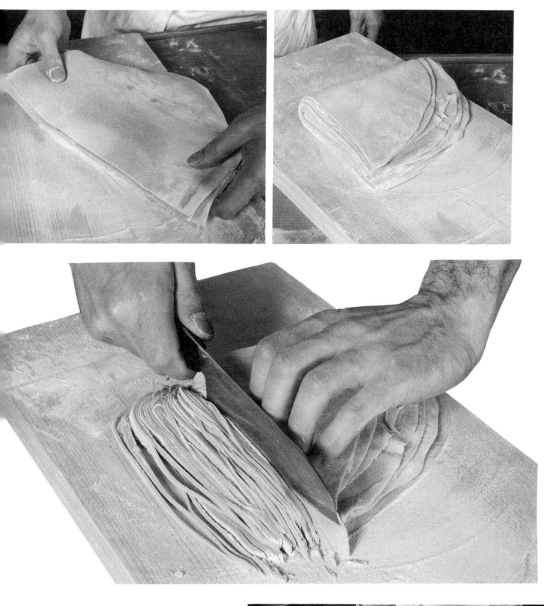

## Cooking the Noodles

When cooking soba noodles use an ample amount of water. As is true of other types of noodles, there is really no such thing as too much water, but too little water may, among other things, cause noodles to cling together or otherwise cook improperly. In general, the following is recommended:

For ¼ pound of noodles use 2 quarts of water
For ½ pound,                2½ quarts
For 1 pound,                4 quarts

Since there is perhaps a limit to the capacity of pots ordinarily at hand, use more than one pot or cook the noodles in batches when cooking large amounts.

In determining whether a pot is too large or small, a rule of thumb suggests the true capacity of a pot to be 80 percent at most. Using these figures and guidelines, make the most suitable adjustments possible within the limits of your cooking vessels. Just keep in mind, the bigger the better.

STEP 1

Bring the water to a rolling boil. Add the noodles and stir gently back and forth, being particularly careful if you are using fresh noodles, since they are more prone to break apart than dry ones.

## STEP 2

Soon after the noodles are put into the water, their starch begins to dissolve. This causes the water to become milky and soon a foam will form and swell to the top.

FOR FRESH NOODLES: Control the foam by lowering the flame. Be ready to lower it to a simmer as soon as the water returns to a boil and before the foam begins to rise. Once lowered, simmer with the water level near to but just shy of the rim for about 1 to 1½ minutes.

FOR DRIED NOODLES: When the water starts to swell, add ½ cup of cold water and lower the heat slightly. Repeat this procedure twice. When the water comes to a boil for the third time, test the noodles (see the next step). If they are done turn off the heat and remove from the stove.

## STEP 3

To test, occasionally lift a few noodles from the pot. Finished noodles should be served *al dente*; that is, tender but firm and chewy throughout. Press or taste noodles frequently. Remember, if the noodles are to be served in a hot broth, they should be slightly undercooked here (and allowed to finish "cooking" in the broth).

## STEP 4

Pour the noodles into a strainer, capturing the cooking water in another pot. Reserve a portion of the cooking water, or *soba-yu* (which contains valuable water-soluble proteins and minerals), if the recipe calls for it. Remove the noodles to a large bowl of cold water to firm up the noodles. When the noodles have cooled somewhat, stir briskly for 5 to 10 seconds to "wash" the starch off. Rinse well.

*homemade soba noodles* • 27

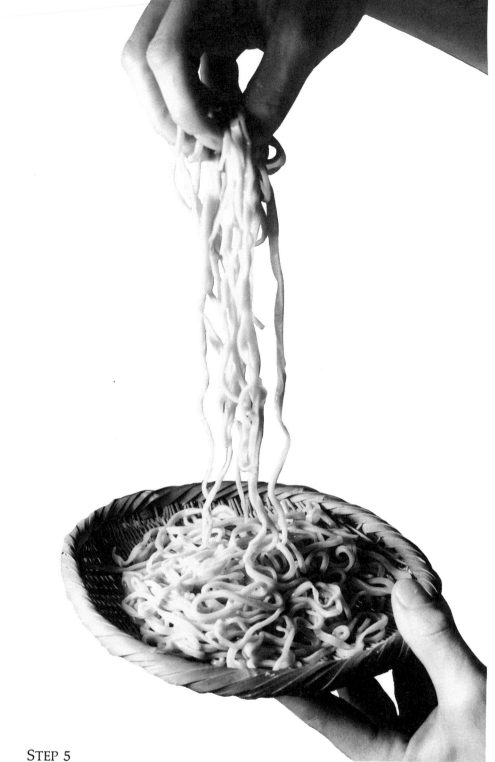

## STEP 5

To cool or chill the noodles, douse in cold water just before serving. Use ice water in summer. Drain well.

To reheat the noodles, place them in a strainer and dip in hot cooking water (reheat if necessary) for 30 to 60 seconds. Drain well.

To serve, follow the instructions for each recipe. If the noodles are to be served on a plate, make sure to drain them well first.

# Broth

Either a hot or cold broth accompanies a portion of soba noodles. A bowl of hot noodles is served in a piping hot broth, a plate or "basket" of cold noodles with a dipping sauce. Aside from the temperature at which they are served (and infinite regional variations), the main difference between the two broths lies in the strength: the cold version has approximately three times the flavor base of its hot counterpart.

The dipping sauce, which developed mainly in the Kanto, or eastern region of Japan (around Tokyo), is served in small portions (usually a small ladleful) in a nicely decorated and rather petite cup known as a *choko*. It has a wonderfully refreshing and stimulating bite that complements the modest but pure, clean taste of buckwheat.

The hot soup, developed mainly in the Kansai, or western region of Japan (around Kyoto and Osaka), is usually served in large bowls with hot soba noodles. As its Kansai nickname, *ama-jiru* (sweet or mild broth), implies, it is meant to be pleasing to the last drop without leaving a salty aftertaste.

It is said that no two soba shops in Japan make exactly the same broth. This belief, exaggerated or not, illustrates the fact that many elements are at play in determining the final taste. Although the two most obvious of these seem to be the quality and ratio of ingredients, other subtle but undeniable factors contribute to the variety of broths. One often-cited factor is the time involved in cooking down the broth. The professionals judge a broth to be done not by how long it has cooked but by how much it has decreased in volume, since the cooking time varies according to the flame, the thickness of the pot, and other variables. From this we can take the hint that it is the volume of stock combined with just the right volume of flavor base that is one of the most fundamental factors in creating a delicious soup to accompany soba.

Four different soba broths are given here, from which you will be able to understand the basics. These recipes represent the standard methods of preparation which have been passed down through the centuries, and yield soups which splendidly complement the taste of soba.

Recipe I—a professional method for making a large quantity of flavor base that can be kept indefinitely and continues to mature the longer it is kept.

Recipe II—a scaled-down version of the first recipe that matures in 6 to 8 hours.

Recipe III—an instant broth.

Recipe IV—a sugarless broth for those on restricted diets.

As you become more comfortable in their preparation, feel free to make adjustments in your search for the taste which best matches your individual or family needs.

For those who are on restricted salt diets, any of the stocks suggested in these recipes will yield a satisfying hot soup. For a saltless chilled soup, allow this same stock to cool and then combine with fresh "in-season" fruit or vegetable juices to suit your dietary needs, or follow the suggestions below.

EXPANDING YOUR REPERTOIRE OF SOBA BROTHS

Although the following recommended broths are traditional favorites, there is no reason why the stock must be limited only to bonito and/or *konbu* kelp. Since the sweet, mild taste of buckwheat is, like tofu, subtle and sophisticated, it lends itself well to almost any combination of ingredients. The main point, after all, is to enhance your diet by eating buckwheat.

Therefore, for those who want to experiment, the field is wide open. If you love chicken soup or beef bouillon, try making your favorite broths and then adding the flavor base at the end.

For variations on the chilled dipping sauce, you might blend it in a food processor together with soft fruits such as avocados or bananas. Or, to attain a nutty fragrance, combine it with walnuts, peanuts, or the like. Try spicing it with ginger or finely chopped celery. Served with chilled fresh noodles, this combination will not only revive almost any flagging appetite but will help to ease those summertime blues.


# RECIPE I

## A Professional Broth

In the soba shop, the master makes his broth or dipping sauce by combining that day's stock with a bit of his own blend of flavor base. He prepares the base days or months in advance and allows it to mature—like good wine.

There are many advantages to making the flavor base and broth separately. Once made and properly stored (storage is described in detail below), the base will keep indefinitely. This enables it to be used with great flexibility and convenience. For example, merely by altering the ratio between the base and the basic stock (also explained below), you can make either the hot soup or the chilled dipping sauce. That is, when you want to make a fresh broth, you need only prepare a basic stock and combine it with the "premade" base. In addition, this method allows you to easily adjust the strength of the soup by simply reducing or increasing the base/stock ratio.

A further advantage is that, having this flavor base on hand, you will find many ways to sneak it into your cooking—for example, using it as a flavoring agent for a teriyaki sauce, brushing it over fried or baked chicken, or adding that "extra" taste to stews, breads, or cooked vegetables.

Another benefit of a separate base is that, as in the fermentation process which takes place in wine- and miso-making, the "edge" (that is, the salt in the soy sauce and the sugar) is softened and allowed to "ferment" for at least 3 days before using (although in a pinch it can be used after 12 hours). Thus, it develops a well-balanced taste and takes on a nature greater than the sum of its parts.

BASE

**Yields 5 cups***

> 1 qt *soy sauce*
> ¾ *cup* mirin
> ⅗ *cup sugar*\* (150 g)

Combine the soy sauce and *mirin* in a heavy-bottomed pot and heat over a medium flame. Take special pains to dry the pot completely with a towel, as even a drop of water will endanger the proper storing ability of this base.

When a white foam starts to form on the surface, add the sugar, lower the flame a touch, and stir continuously with a wooden spoon to prevent the sugar from sticking to the bottom. The sugar will dissolve and the white foam will again begin to form. When it covers about 50 percent of the surface (professionals will allow it to go to 80 or 90 percent), remove the pot from the stove. Although it is permissible to allow the liquid to boil slightly at the rim, watch it closely and do not let it reach a full boil.

Since this base is going to be used over a long period of time, it is essential that not even a hint of water be allowed to enter into the process at any point. Before placing it in a storage container, allow the base to sit overnight in a cool, dark place. Cover with a cloth, towel, or newspaper (water will condense on a pot lid or other nonabsorbent cover).

At the traditional shops this base is allowed to mature and mellow for 3 full days before using. As the quantities called for in this recipe are tailored to a home scale, a minimum maturing period of 12 hours (overnight) is more than sufficient, although 2 to 3 days will produce a superior flavor.

Store in a covered container in a cool, dark place.

\*Combined with the recommended stock, the flavor base in this recipe will provide enough soup for 68 portions of cold dipping sauce or about 30 portions of the hot variety (depending on the strength). This means that there will only be about 2.2 grams of sugar in a portion of the chilled soup and about 5 grams in a portion of the hot.

## Making the Stock

As stocks using *konbu* kelp will cloud if allowed to sit for more than 24 hours, make only as much stock as you will use on that day. Nevertheless, these recipes will all yield slightly more than the "standard volume," to ensure that you will not come up short.

HOT STOCK

Serves 6

    4–6 *inch length* konbu *kelp*
        *(optional)*
    8 *cups water*
    1½–2 *oz bonito flakes*

CHILLED STOCK

    2 *inch length* konbu *kelp*
        *(optional)*
    1½ *cups water*
    ⅔–1 *oz bonito flakes*

Wipe the kelp lightly with a dry cloth and combine with water in a wide-mouthed pot. Cook over a low heat for 3 minutes. To ensure a thicker and tastier broth, leave the kelp in for 1 to 2 minutes after the broth reaches a boil. Then remove it and turn up the heat to medium-high.

When the stock starts to boil in earnest, add the bonito flakes. Skim off the white foam and continue boiling over a low heat for about 10 to 15 minutes.

When the stock has boiled down to about two-thirds of its original volume, turn off the flame. In one motion, pour the broth into a cloth-covered strainer. If you do this too slowly, the fragrance of the bonito is said to diminish noticeably.

At this point, there are two schools of thought. In standard Japanese cooking, to prevent the slightly astringent, "fishy" taste of the bonito from dominating, the cloth containing the wet flakes is not wrung out. Yet, this quality is actually desired by the soba-maker, and hence by and large the practice of thoroughly squeezing the cooked flakes occurs. Experiment and decide which method you want to follow.

## Making the Broth

The stock and flavor base are combined in ratios that have been passed down through the centuries. For those who find the results too weak or strong, however, feel free to make suitable adjustments.

HOT BROTH

    1 *part flavor base*
    8–10 *parts stock*

DIPPING SAUCE

    1 *part flavor base*
    3 *parts stock*

Combine stock and base in required amounts. Heat over a medium-high flame until the broth *starts* to boil at the rim of the pot. Reduce the heat immediately and simmer for 10 to 15 minutes. If you are making hot broth, it is ready to be served at this point.

The chilled dipping sauce, however, obviously must be cooled before serving. This can be done in two ways. The best way is to allow it to cool naturally for about 2 to 3 hours, and then cover and refrigerate it until it reaches about 50°F or, in summertime, 40°F. (As in the maturing process of the flavor base, the chilled broth is said to "ripen to its fullest" if allowed to cool naturally.) When time is short, the broth can be "force-cooled" after it has been allowed to cool naturally for about 10 minutes. To do this, place the pot of broth in a larger pot or bowl filled with ice water and stir until it reaches the above temperature.

## RECIPE II

## A Professional Broth at Home

Here is a professional recipe that can be made on a smaller scale. Although the basic principle is the same as in Recipe I, by practicing with the lesser amounts given here, you can gain confidence and also determine what adjustments (if any) you would like to make to the standard recipe before making the larger amount of flavor base. In addition, since the scale is smaller, the flavor base will mature quicker and be ready to serve 6 to 8 hours after making. Therefore, you could make it in the morning for an evening soba party.

FLAVOR BASE

**Yields about 9 cups\***

> 1½  cups soy sauce
>
> ¼  cup mirin
>
> ¼  cup sugar

COLD FLAVOR BASE

> 2⅛ cups soy sauce
>
> 7  Tbsps mirin
>
> 6  Tbsps sugar

STOCK

> 7½  cups water
>
> 1½–3  oz bonito flakes

Make the flavor base following the instructions in the previous recipe. Allow to mature for 6 to 8 hours. Combine the broth ingredients following the procedure given in Recipe I (omitting the steps for *konbu* kelp).

## RECIPE III

## Instant Broth

This recipe is easier and quicker than the first two, but has been placed last so that by now you will thoroughly understand the principal do's and don'ts of making a successful soba soup. Although it is meant for immediate use, this broth, like the flavor bases of the earlier recipes, benefits if it is allowed to sit for a time, in this case overnight.

CHILLED DIPPING SAUCE

> 5 inch piece konbu *kelp*
>
> ½ cup soy sauce
>
> 2 cups water
>
> 2–3 oz bonito flakes
>
> 3½ Tbsps mirin
>
> 2½ Tbsps sugar

HOT BROTH

> 5 inch piece konbu *kelp*
>
> 8 cups water
>
> 3–4 oz bonito flakes
>
> 1 cup soy sauce
>
> 5 Tbsps mirin
>
> 4 Tbsps sugar

Wipe the kelp with a damp cloth and place in the water. Bring the water to a boil at a high heat.

When the water comes to a boil, remove the kelp and immediately add the bonito flakes. Reduce the heat to medium and allow the water to boil for 3 minutes, stirring and pushing down the flakes with a wooden spoon.

Reduce to a low flame and add the soy sauce, *mirin*, and sugar. Cook for an additional 5 minutes. Stir gently to prevent the sugar from sticking to the bottom and to bring out the full taste of the bonito flakes.

Pour the finished broth through a cloth-covered strainer.

# RECIPE IV

## A Sugarless Broth

> 1 oz bonito flakes
>
> 4 cups water
>
> 1 cup soy sauce
>
> 1 cup mirin

Place the bonito and water in a pot and heat over a high flame.

When the broth starts to boil, a white foam will form on the surface. Skim off the foam and lower the heat to medium-low for about 2 minutes. The flame should be just hot enough to keep the flakes aloft and moving around.

Pour through a cloth-covered strainer, then return to the stove. Turn the flame to high. When the broth begins to boil at the rim of the pot, add the soy sauce and *mirin*. Return to a boil, turn off the heat, and remove the pot from the stove.

For the hot broth, serve as is. For the chilled broth, allow to cool as for standard dipping sauce (page 32).

# The Professional Method

*The three main steps of mixing, rolling, and cutting are the same in both the professional and home methods. At the professional shop, a lacquered mixing bowl is used to give a nice smooth finish to the ball of dough. A fine cypress roller and two longer wrapping pins are used to handle the large sheet of dough. A tall knife like the one shown on the title page is used in combination with a board (komaita) to ensure even cutting through 12 to 16 or as many as 20 layers of dough.*

1

2

3

4

5

6

7

8

9

10

11

12

13

14

15

16

17

18

19

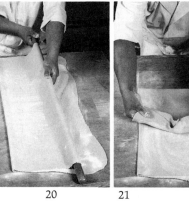

20

21

22

23

# NOODLE
# DISHES

Soba Noodles in a Basket

"Rosy-Cheeked" Soba

Front to back: Duck and Leek Soba (see Chicken and Leek Soba), Soba Noodles with Whipped Mountain Yam and Egg, "Fox" Soba.

39

# COUNTRY COOKING

Wanko Soba Party with Tempura

# SOBA COURSE

Front to back: Soba Dumpling with Miso Sauce, Soba Sushi, Soba-Sesame Tofu, Kasha with Mixed Vegetables, Mixed-fry Tempura in a Soba Broth (*nuki*), Soba Noodles, Toasted Nori Seaweed (dusted with buckwheat flour).

# NOODLE DISHES

Cold Soba Noodles with
Natto and Sesame

Curry Soba

Tempura Soba

Front to back: Soba Noodles with
Tempura, Cold Soba Noodles with
Grated Radish, Soba Salad.

# GROAT COOKING

Groat and Mountain Yam Fry

Soba Groat Zosui

Kasha with Pickles

# VARIATIONS

Foreground: Soba Pasty, Saké-seasoned Soba Patties, Soba Mochi Squares. Pit: Stew with Soba Dumplings, Soba Dumplings with Miso Sauce (light and dark flour).

Front to back: Soba Sushi, Soba-
Sesame Tofu, Soba Crepe.

# STAGES OF SOBA

Whole seed, flour, and dried noodles.

# JAPANESE FOODS

All of the items here are available at major food markets or Japanese food outlets. See the Ingredients section for explanations. Figures in parentheses correspond to packaged and bottled goods at the bottom of the facing page.

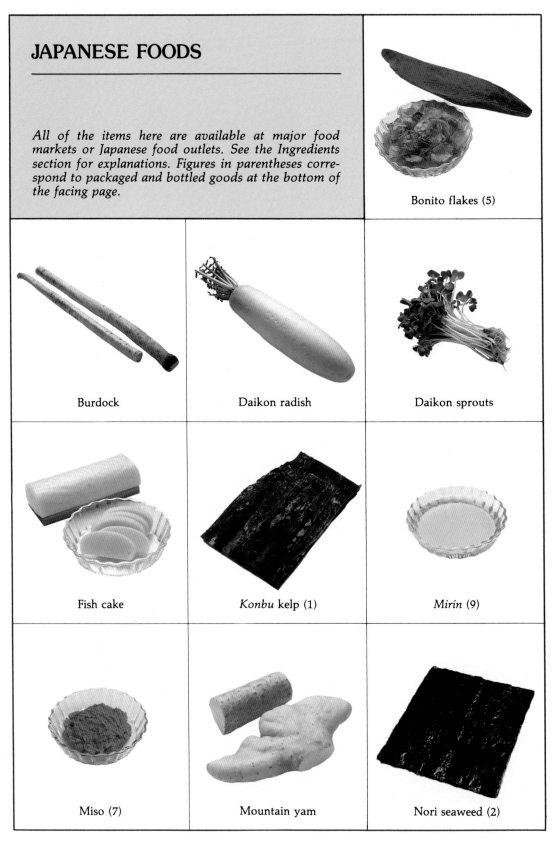

Bonito flakes (5)

Burdock

Daikon radish

Daikon sprouts

Fish cake

*Konbu* kelp (1)

*Mirin* (9)

Miso (7)

Mountain yam

Nori seaweed (2)

Salmon roe

Seven-spice pepper (8)

Shiitake mushrooms (4)

*Shiso* leaves

Soba noodles, dried,
regular and green-tea (6)

Soy sauce, light
and regular (11)

Tofu, fresh and
thin deep-fried

*Wakame* seaweed (3)

*Wasabi* horseradish (10)

# BUCKWHEAT—
# FROM FIELD TO FLOUR

A field of buckwheat in bloom.

Harvested buckwheat stacked to dry.

Emerging buckwheat seeds

Maturing seeds

Buckwheat flower

# BUCKWHEAT FLOUR

*Sarashina* flour          No. 1 flour          No. 2 flour          No. 3 flour

Dark flour (*sanago*)     *Uchiko* flour     Cracked groats, fine grade  Cracked groats, coarse

# SERVING WARE

Trays (*seiro, zaru*)

Bowls (*donburi*)

Dipping cups (*choko*)

Sauce bottles (*tokkuri*)

Pitchers for *soba-yu* (*yuto*)

Condiment containers

# TOOLS

Mixing bowl

Rolling pins

Knife

# SOBA RESTAURANTS

In the act of lifting the soba from her bowl, a geisha pauses to gaze at a sparrow in flight. (A *ukiyo-e* print by Utagawa Toyokuni III, ca. 1820–40)

Soba even found its way into Kabuki. Here the villain contemplates his next move over a bowl of "two-eight" noodles at a night stand. (Utagawa Toyokuni III)

Tokyo soba shop, exterior view.

Soba shop with rich, wood interior.

Take Yabu, Kashiwa (near Tokyo).

52

# Noodle Dishes

## Soba Noodles in a Basket                    *Mori/Zaru/Seiro Soba*

This is the simplest and yet "most dangerous" dish on the soba master's menu. It is also the most popular. Since only the dipping sauce and the humblest of garnishes accompany it, the noodle must stand on its own merits. To the connoisseur of soba, this is the most delicious way—some say the only way—to savor buckwheat's sweetness. *Mori Soba* and the nori-topped *Zaru Soba* are extremely popular on a hot summer day, and interestingly enough, are often served at the end of a banquet or party-style dinners where the guests have had a lot to drink. Not only does soba help to lower the blood pressure but it also aids the liver in dealing with alcohol. Combining the cooking water, which contains much of the water-soluble protein, with the remaining dipping sauce to make a soup is a satisfying final touch.

The roots of the Japanese name of this dish reach back to well over three hundred years ago to a time when the work of making soba noodles was entrusted to the local confectioner. Since noodles made from one-hundred percent buckwheat are prone to break easily, sweets makers steamed and then served the noodles in bamboo baskets, or *take zaru*. Though today wheat flour mixed in with the buckwheat gives the dough a binding power that makes it possible to boil the noodles, the tradition of putting them out on bamboo baskets continues, and so does the name.

1¼  lbs homemade soba noodles
    or
  1  lb dried soba noodles
1¾  cups dipping sauce
    or
  7  Tbsps flavor base and 1¼
    cups stock
  1  sheet nori seaweed (optional),
    cut into thin strips
  2  scallions, finely sliced
  2  tsps wasabi horseradish
  4  Tbsps grated daikon radish

**Serves 4**

Make the dipping sauce of your choice (pages 29–34) and chill it (page 32).

Boil and wash the noodles (page 26), reserving about one-third of the cooking water. Drain well.

Place the noodles on plates or in traditional *zaru* baskets and garnish with strips of nori. Set out the dipping sauce for each person. Season sauce to taste with scallion, *wasabi*, and grated daikon. Serve immediately.

When you have finished eating the noodles, reheat the cooking water and top off the remaining dipping sauce to make a soup.

## Hot Soba Noodles in a Broth            *Kake Soba*

This is hot soba at its most basic. Originally served with a lukewarm soup as a quick, nutritious meal for hurried laborers and craftsmen of the early seventeenth century, this simple and satisfying meal still enjoys an immense following among those on the run. Try topping the noodles with a quarter sheet of nori seaweed crowned with salmon roe caviar (*ikura*).

1¼ lbs homemade soba noodles
    or
1 lb dried soba noodles
6 cups broth
    or
1½ cups flavor base and 4½
    cups stock
1½ Tbsps grated ginger
2 scallions, finely sliced

**Serves 4**

Make the broth of your choice (pages 29–34).

Boil, wash, and reheat the noodles (page 26), but remove them before they are *al dente*. The noodles should be about 90 percent done (they will finish cooking when placed in the hot broth). Wash and strain, then set aside in a strainer.

Reheat the broth over a high heat and at the same time reheat the cooking water. When the broth shows the first signs of boiling at the rim of the pot, remove from heat. Reheat the noodles one portion at a time by placing in strainer and dipping in the hot cooking water.

Place the noodles in serving bowls. Cover with the hot broth, garnish with ginger and scallion, and serve immediately.

VARIATION: A simpler recipe for hot noodles calls for the noodles to be served in their steaming-hot cooking water, which contains many dissolved proteins and other nutrients. The noodles are dipped in a hot dipping sauce with a 5 to 1 ratio of stock to flavor base.

## Cold Soba Noodles with Grated Radish

This dish is particularly refreshing on a sultry summer afternoon. The zesty daikon (choose as spicy a one as you can find) serves to whet flagging appetites. Don't hold back on the bonito flakes or ground sesame, the latter of which lessens the slight astringency of the flakes.

1¼ lbs homemade soba noodles
   or
1 lb dried soba noodles
1¾ cups dipping sauce
   or
7 Tbsps flavor base and 1¼
   cups stock
2 tsps fresh sesame seeds
2 cups grated daikon radish
   (substitute any large white
   radish)
2 scallions, finely sliced
1 sheet nori seaweed, toasted
   and shredded
4 heaping Tbsps bonito flakes
   Soy sauce

**Serves 4**

Make the broth of your choice (pages 29–34) and cool (page 32).

Toast the sesame seeds in a dry frypan over medium heat until they begin to emit a nutlike fragrance, then remove *immediately* from the pan. Grind with a mortar and pestle.

Boil, wash, and cool the noodles (page 26), reserving the water.

Drain the noodles well and place in individual serving bowls. Squeeze out excess water from the grated radish, then mound on top of the noodles. Sprinkle the scallion, nori, bonito flakes, and finally sesame around the daikon. Pour a small amount of soy sauce over the radish. Set out individual portions of dipping sauce. Add sliced scallions to sauce as desired. When you have finished the noodles, reheat the cooking water and top off the remaining sauce to make a soup.

## Tempura Soba

Ask any master of a high-class soba restaurant what the most popular dish on his menu is, and most likely Tempura Soba will get the nod. Basically there are three types, each a variation along the soba noodle–tempura axis.

The most common version calls for large shrimp to be dipped in tempura batter and deep-fried, tail and all. These are set right on top of a bed of hot noodles floating in broth. Another type combines shrimp or assorted tempura with Soba Noodles in a Basket, and is called *Tenzaru*. (To make this simply follow this recipe but serve the noodles cold with a dipping sauce. The tempura becomes a side dish.) The last variety is an attractive mixed-fry tempura "patty." This is likewise set on top of hot noodles or served on its own tray when accompanying cold noodles (see the following recipe).

The style you choose to serve will of course be influenced by your or your guest's preference but generally first timers seem to like the tempura served on its own separate dish, as it retains its crispy quality. Yet for others, the rich taste and body-warming feeling that is produced by allowing the tempura to melt into the soup is more desirable.

With any of these, the tempura should be served almost immediately after cooking. If it is allowed to sit for more than 2 or 3 minutes, its crispiness is lost. Ideally, the tempura should be hot enough to make a sizzling, crackling sound as it is placed into the hot broth. At high-class restaurants this sizzling sound will still be audible when it is placed in front of you! Take a hint from the soba master's showmanship, and try to strike a balance between practicality and a respect for the tempura.

**Serves 4**

1¼ lbs homemade soba noodles
    or
 1 lb dried soba noodles
6½ cups hot broth
    or
 10 Tbsps flavor base and 6 cups
    stock

TEMPURA*
 8 large shrimp
1½ cups all-purpose flour
 1 cup cold water
 1 egg yolk
    Oil for deep-frying

Make the broth of your choice (pages 29–34).

Prepare the shrimp: Remove the outer shell, trim the middle prong of the tail but leave the 2 outer ones. Rinse the shrimp in salt water. Devein by making a lengthwise insertion along the back and removing the blackish material with a toothpick. Make 3 shallow incisions horizontally along the underside so that the cooked shrimp will lay flat (that is, it will not curl up when placed in the oil). Run the dull edge of the knife along the tail to force out any excess water from the tail fins. Pat the shrimp dry.

Combine the egg yolk with 1 cup water and whip briskly for about 3 to 5 seconds. Sift in the flour and stir gently in a "figure 8" 2 or 3 times. This will be enough to ensure a proper blending. The final batter should look incompletely mixed. Too much stirring will activate the gluten within the wheat and create a sticky, pastelike batter, which is not suitable for making good tempura. (The technique in mixing the batter is similar to that of the tofu maker's method of stirring *nigari* into the heated soybean juice: the idea is not to disturb.) Therefore, stop mixing while a ring of flour still remains around the rim.

If the batter drips off the fork in noticeably distinct drops, it is the proper consistency. It shouldn't run off like water, nor should it just stick there.

The proper temperature of the oil can be tested by putting a drop or two of the batter into the oil. If the drop sinks to the bottom, the oil is still too cold. If the first few drops stay on top as soon as they make contact, the oil is too hot. Therefore, the proper temperature is attained when the few drops of batter sink down almost to the bottom and come right up (320°–360°F). Adjust the flame until the proper heat is attained.

Meanwhile, boil and wash the noodles (page 26). Remove to a strainer. Reserve the cooking water to reheat the noodles.

When the noodles are finished, begin the tempura. Pick up the prepared shrimp by holding the tail end with the first two fingers and thumb of either hand. Dip it briefly but completely into the batter, then transfer it quickly but gently to the oil. Cook until the outside is crispy and golden yellow (not brown). The inside, of course, should be cooked but not hard.

While the tempura is cooking, reheat the broth. Remove it from the stove as soon as it begins to boil at the rim.

Reheat the noodles, place them in individual bowls, cover with hot broth, and top with the shrimp. Serve immediately.

*Soba shops use a batter that is slightly thicker than standard tempura batter, so it is allowed to cook a little longer in the oil. Depending on whether someone comes from the Tokyo or Osaka area, their opinion as to what is the best kind of oil will differ. Tokyo style calls for the richer (and more expensive) sesame oil as a base (20 percent). Osaka style relies on a light vegetable oil.

The key point to obtaining a successful tempura is to perform all of the various activities quickly and confidently, so that the noodles will not be finished too far in advance of the tempura, and absolutely not vice versa.

As for the cooking time, please keep in mind that the ingredients to be deep-fried should be so fresh that they can be eaten raw (or nearly so). This is the unspoken assumption of all good tempura chefs. Thus, even if the tempura is a little bit "undercooked," it is not at all a total failure, since the food could have been eaten as it was. By following this practice you need only guard against overcooking. Tempura is meant to be delicate, so avoid a hard, dark-colored finished product.

Incidentally, the professionals judge the tempura not only by sight, but also by sound. During the first half-minute or so of deep-frying, the tempura will make a sizzling sound. When it is sufficiently cooked, the sound will become a crackling chorus. When you can distinguish between the two, you will know that your tempura-making ability has progressed.

## Soba Noodles with Mixed-Fry Tempura

This recipe features a patty-shaped tempura and calls for shrimp and scallops, though very often only shrimp are used. The easiest way to prepare this dish is simply to put all the chopped ingredients directly into a rather thick batter and then spoon the mixture into preheated oil (320°–360°F). A second, more sophisticated method which produces a much lighter result is also described below.

**Serves 4**

1¼ lbs homemade soba noodles
or
1 lb dried soba noodles

6½ cups hot broth
or

10 Tbsps flavor base and 6 cups stock

2 scallions, finely sliced

TEMPURA

½ lb shrimp

3 oz very fresh scallops

<pre>
½  medium onion, chopped
    Oil for deep-frying
1½  cups all-purpose flour
  1  egg yolk
  1  cup water
</pre>

Make the broth of your choice (pages 29–34).

Wash and devein the shrimp. Remove the tails. Wash the scallops in lightly salted water. Chop both coarsely.

Boil and wash the noodles (page 26). Reserve the cooking water.

Preheat the oil. To test the temperature of the oil, see the previous recipe.

Make the batter following the instructions in the previous recipe. In a separate bowl, combine the shrimp, scallops, and chopped onion. Follow one of the two methods for deep-frying.

METHOD A: This is the easiest of the two. Thicken the batter with 2 to 3 Tbsps of flour. Then ladle one-fourth of the chopped ingredients directly into the batter and coat well. Scoop out a "patty" of seafood with a spatula and place it into the oil. Shape the patty by dripping extra batter on top and mounding on any stray pieces. Cook to a light golden color (not brown).

METHOD B: This is a more sophisticated way (used by the professionals) and produces a lighter tempura. Find an empty can. It should be about 4 inches in diameter. Cut out the ends, then wash and dry it well. Place it in the preheated oil. Add the chopped ingredients to the batter, mix, and then ladle into the can. Drip a few drops of batter on top, creating a nice "crown" effect. Spoon about 4 or 5 ladles of oil over the top and cook for about 30 seconds. Lift the can from the tempura and cook until the batter turns a light golden color. Repeat this procedure to make 3 more patties. Before making the remaining patties, test the oil. The patty shape should form within about 10 to 15 seconds and become firm within 30 seconds. Cook about 2 to 3 minutes. Allow the finished tempura to drain for about 5 to 10 seconds before serving.

Reheat the broth. Reheat the noodles by placing them in a strainer and dipping them in hot cooking water. Shake out the extra water, and place them in individual bowls. Cover with the broth, crown with the tempura, garnish with scallion, and serve immediately.

## Soba Noodles with Whipped Mountain Yam and Egg

The Japanese mountain yam is undeniably an acquired taste, but once acquired, like many another fine food, it is addicting. It is cool and refreshing and as slippery as oysters in a half shell. Western palates will find the glutinous stickiness of the yam yet another one of those inexplicable Japanese culinary experiences. It has a mild taste, so it responds well when combined with other foods or seasonings, such as the broth in this recipe.

<pre>
1¼  lbs fresh soba noodles
       or
  1  lb dried soba noodles
</pre>

**Serves 4**

1¾ *cups dipping sauce*
*or*
7 *Tbsps flavor base and 1¼
cups stock*

1 *medium mountain yam
(yama imo)*

1 *sheet nori seaweed*

4 *egg yolks (optional)*

2 *scallions, finely sliced*

2 *tsps* wasabi *horseradish*

Make the dipping sauce of your choice (pages 29–34) and chill (page 31).

Pour half of the chilled sauce into a bowl, and grate half of the yam. Repeat with the remaining broth and yam. Combine both portions and mix well.

Toast the seaweed by passing it back and forth over a high flame several times until it becomes shiny. Tear into bite-sized pieces.

Boil, wash, and strain the noodles (page 26).

Place the noodles in individual bowls. Cup your hand over the noodles and turn the bowl upside down, gently pressing the noodles to squeeze out any remaining water. Top with the grated yam and crown with an egg yolk (if desired). Garnish with nori, scallion, and *wasabi*. Serve immediately. Mix well before eating.

## Cold Soba Noodles with Natto and Sesame

*Natto*, a kind of fermented soybean product, has a somewhat strong fragrance and flavor somewhat similar to that of fine cheese. But when "garnished" with the chilled soba broth, the combination exhibits an exotic, almost burgundylike fragrance and taste which complements buckwheat's modest sweetness. The recipe itself is very easy, but it is important to achieve a proper balance between the *natto*, the other garnishes, and the chilled dipping sauce.

1¼ *lbs homemade soba noodles*
*or*
1 *lb dried soba noodles*

1¾ *cups dipping sauce*
*or*
7 *Tbsps flavor base and 1¼
cups stock*

⅔ *oz natto*

2 *scallions, finely sliced*

4 *egg yolks (optional)*

4 *tsps fresh sesame seeds*

1 *sheet nori seaweed*

4 *heaping tsps bonito flakes*

**Serves 4**

Make the dipping sauce (pages 29–34) and chill (page 32).

When working with *natto*, its dual nature should be taken into account. On the one hand, *natto* is made from cooked soybeans, which are inherently sweet. Yet, when these cooked soybeans are activated with a fermenting seed and allowed to sit at slightly above room temperature for about 16 to 24 hours, the outer part of the bean takes on a mild, astringent taste, while the center part retains its sweetness. Therefore, if you are not accustomed to the astringent side of *natto*, you probably would like to bring out the sweetness of the soybeans as much as possible.

METHOD A (to bring out the sweetness): Use a dry cutting board. To guarantee stability, place a damp towel underneath it. With a heavy knife dice the *natto* to create a very fine glutinous texture. Spend 1 to 2 minutes chopping with quick, brisk strokes. Don't be discouraged by *natto*'s stickiness. It is not necessary that the knife be pulled completely free of the beans on the upstroke. The important thing is to thoroughly mash them.

METHOD B: Chop the *natto* briskly for about 20 to 30 seconds into a coarse mix. This activates the *natto* just enough to make it more digestible, but not too much to destroy the biting effect, which is what real *natto* lovers crave.

Whip the *natto* together into a ball.

Place the sesame seeds in a dry skillet over a low heat. Roast, stirring constantly until the seeds begin to emit a nutlike fragrance. Remove immediately from the pan. Grind in a mortar and pestle.

Pass the sheet of nori seaweed back and forth over a medium flame several times. Within 10 to 15 seconds, the surface will become shiny and the nori will emit a nice fragrance. Turn off the heat and tear the sheet into bite-sized pieces.

Boil, wash, and rinse the noodles (page 26).

Place the noodles in individual bowls, and with one hand cupped over the top, turn the bowl upside down and gently press to squeeze out any excess water. Add ¼ cup broth. Make a small indentation in the center of the noodles, and then place an egg yolk in the hole. Garnish with the nori, bonito flakes, and sliced onions. Top with *natto*, then sprinkle sesame seeds over the *natto*. To eat, mix the ingredients, combining well with the broth.

## "Rosy-Cheeked" Soba *Okame Soba*

This dish was inspired by the image of the robust working woman of two hundred years past, or so it is said. Colorful ingredients are playfully arranged to suggest a woman's face. Pink or pink-bordered slices of fish cake recall their glowing cheeks. Substitute freely with whatever you have on hand: sliced carrots for fish cake, spinach for daikon radish sprouts, and so on. If possible cover the dish before you serve it to create an element of mystery. When the lid is lifted, a fine steam unveils a display of delicate garnishes artfully arranged.

1¼ *lbs homemade soba noodles*
  *or*
1 *lb dried soba noodles*
7 *cups hot broth*
  *or*
11 *Tbsps flavor base and 6½ cups stock*
5 *Tbsps soy sauce*

**Serves 4**

    2 *Tbsps* mirin

    2 *tsps sugar (optional)*

THE FACE

    4 *shrimp (hair)*

    1½ *oz bamboo shoots (eyes)*

    4 *fresh mushrooms (nose)*

    3 *eggs (mouth)*

    8 *slices fish cake* (kamaboko)

    8 *carrot rounds (cheeks)*

    16 *strands daikon radish
        sprouts (bow)*

Make the broth of your choice (pages 29–34).

Wash and devein the shrimp. Boil for 1 minute.

Cut the bamboo shoots into bite-sized pieces. Remove the stems from the mushrooms. Combine the soy sauce, *mirin*, and sugar with 1 cup broth. Place the mushrooms and bamboo shoots in separate pots and add a portion of broth mixture to each. Bring to a boil and then simmer uncovered until the liquid is absorbed (about 10 minutes).

Add 1½ Tbsps flavor base and 3 Tbsps stock to the eggs. Mix roughly, as you would with tempura batter, since you want a soft, delicate texture. Preheat a skillet over medium heat. Lightly oil the pan and add half of the egg. Tap the egg mixture lightly, using chopsticks (or thin shish-kabob-type skewers) to encourage air bubbles to form. When the heat has penetrated but the egg is still moist and runny, fold in thirds. Slide it to the front of the pan, re-oil the pan, and pour in the remaining egg. Lift the cooked egg so that some of the uncooked egg runs under. Cook and then roll up as before. Form into a bar shape by pressing with a spatula. Cut into ½-inch-wide slices. (If you are in a hurry, substitute egg yolks. Place them in the steaming-hot broth just before serving so that the yolks are soft-poached by the soup.)

Slice the fish cake with the tip of the knife, cutting into pieces about ½ inch thick. By jiggling the knife as you slice, you can make appealing designs.

Boil, wash, and reheat the noodles (page 26).

Place the noodles in individual bowls and make the face. Reheat the broth and pour it into the bowl, being careful not to disturb the garnishes. Serve immediately.

## Soba Noodles with Tempura Crispies             *Tanuki Soba*

This dish features deep-fried "crispies," those stray bits of tempura batter that skitter across the oil during the deep-frying. Even so, the shrimp or other tempura ingredients impart some of their flavor to these wayfarers, so leftover crispies work well here. If you do not plan to make tempura in the near future, however, the crispies can be made to order.

Nowadays, people naturally assume that the dish was originally named after the raccoon dog, whose statue is often found at soba shops. But this is not the case. Originally, the Japanese name for the dish was *Tane-nuki Soba*. The word *tane-nuki* means "ingredients taken out," and referred, of course, to the tempura batter sans ingredients. The Japanese are fond of punning, and it wasn't long before someone thought to drop the second syllable and call it *Tanuki Soba*, or "Raccoon Dog Soba." Since the raccoon dog is characterized as being a sly and stealthy forager, the humorous, if oblique, reference to shrimpless tempura has stuck.

<table>
<tr><td>1¼</td><td>lbs homemade soba noodles<br>or</td></tr>
<tr><td>1</td><td>lb dried soba noodles</td></tr>
<tr><td>6½</td><td>cups hot broth<br>or</td></tr>
<tr><td>10</td><td>Tbsps flavor base and 6 cups stock</td></tr>
<tr><td>8</td><td>oz chicken (optional)</td></tr>
<tr><td>1–2</td><td>scallions, sliced</td></tr>
<tr><td>1</td><td>sheet nori seaweed</td></tr>
<tr><td>4</td><td>bits citron or lemon zest (optional)</td></tr>
</table>

**Serves 4**

BATTER (if necessary)

*Oil for deep-frying*

2   *Tbsps water*

¼   *cup all-purpose white flour*

1   *egg yolk*

If you do not have leftover crispies, make up a fresh batch. Preheat the oil to a medium-low deep-frying temperature (340°F). Mix the batter ingredients roughly (see Tempura Soba, page 55) and ladle into the oil. During the 1 or 2 minutes of cooking, lightly knock the clumps apart, as small, individual pieces are better. When they attain a nice yellow-golden (not brown) color, scoop them out of the oil and drain on absorbent paper.

Make the broth of your choice (pages 29–34). Heat over a high flame until it begins to boil at the outer rim. Turn off the heat.

Boil, wash, and strain the noodles (page 26), keeping the boiling water on hand.

Cut the chicken into bite-sized pieces. Slice the scallion at a diagonal into bite-sized pieces.

Pass the sheet of nori back and forth over a gas flame several times. To avoid burning, keep the nori in a constant waving motion. Within 10 to 15 seconds, the surface will become shiny and the nori will emit a nice fragrance. Turn off the heat and tear the nori into bite-sized pieces.

Reheat the broth until it begins to boil lightly at the rim of the pot, then add the chicken. When the meat rises to the surface, put in the onion. Cook for 30 seconds, then turn off the flame.

Reheat the noodles by placing them in a strainer and dipping them in the cooking water. (Reheat if necessary.) Put the noodles in individual serving bowls, arrange the chicken and onions (bunched together) on top of the noodles, and cover with the steaming broth. Sprinkle with the nori and garnish with the zest. As the "crispies" soon become soft in the soup broth, add them just before you sit down to eat.

## "Fox" Soba

*Kitsune Soba*

This dish takes its name from an old Japanese folk tale which depicts the fox's keen liking for the simple but delicious squares of deep-fried tofu. Light and absorbent, they become juicy, broth-filled morsels when simmered as is done here.

**Serves 4**

1¼  *lbs homemade soba noodles*
     *or*
  1  *lb dried soba noodles*
6½  *cups hot broth*
     *or*
 10  *Tbsps flavor base and 6 cups stock*
  4  *pieces thin deep-fried tofu (abura-age or usu-age)*
2½  *Tbsps soy sauce*
  1  *Tbsp mirin*
  1  *tsp sugar (optional)*
  2  *leeks*
  2  *scallions, finely sliced*

Make the broth of your choice (pages 29–34).

Boil the tofu for about 2 minutes to remove the excess oil. Discard the water. Add hot water to cover, but not so much that the tofu floats. Turn up the flame and boil for 10 minutes. Again, discard the water.

Add the soy sauce, *mirin*, sugar, and ½ cup broth to the tofu and simmer for about 20 minutes or until the broth is absorbed. While the pieces are hot, open them up, stack them on top of each other, and press down to ensure that they lie flat later. (If you wait until they cool off, they will shrivel up.) Allow to cool, then cut into triangles.

Boil, wash, and reheat the noodles (page 26). Place each portion in its own bowl. Reheat the broth until it begins to boil at the rim, then add the leeks and allow to cook until tender.

Peel the outer skin from the leeks. Cut diagonally into thin slices. Place the leeks and deep-fried tofu triangles on top of the noodles and cover with the steaming broth. Garnish with the scallion.

VARIATION WITH THICK DEEP-FRIED TOFU

Boil the thick tofu (*atsu-age*) for 2 to 3 minutes to remove the excess oil. Puncture the whole outer surface of the tofu with a fork or toothpick.

Put the tofu in a pan and add just enough broth to cover. Add the soy sauce, *mirin*, and sugar and turn the flame up high. As the liquid approaches a boil, turn down the heat and simmer for 20 minutes. As the broth goes down, shake the pan occasionally so that it will be evenly absorbed. Remove from the stove and cut into triangles. Serve as above.

# Hot Soba Noodles with Egg Royale     *Kakitama Soba*

This soba dish features a soft, puddinglike broth obtained by first thickening the broth with either potato or *kuzu* starch just previous to stirring in the lightly whipped eggs.

There are several other equally popular egg dishes. *Toji Soba* calls for well-whipped eggs to be added instead of the starch just as the broth comes to a boil. Moon-viewing Soba, or *Tsukimi Soba*, dispenses with a thickening agent altogether. Rather, a raw egg is nestled in the center of the noodles and boiling soup broth is poured over it, softly poaching the egg and creating a thin, misty surface, hence its name.

**Serves 4**

1¼ lbs homemade soba noodles
  or
1 lb dried soba noodles

6½ cups hot broth
  or
10 Tbsps flavor base and 6 cups stock

1 bunch spinach

4 eggs

2 heaping Tbsps potato starch (katakuriko) or kuzu or 3 generous Tbsps cornstarch

4 slices fish cake (kamaboko) (optional)

4 tsps grated ginger

2–3 scallions, finely sliced

4 shiso leaves, chopped (optional)

Make the broth of your choice (pages 29–34).

Cook the spinach and place it in cold water to preserve the color.

Boil and wash the noodles (page 26). While waiting for the water to boil, combine the starch with enough water (about ¼ cup) to achieve a gravylike texture. Stir until the texture is smooth and all of the lumps dissolve. In a separate bowl, lightly whip the eggs together.

Heat the broth over a high flame. When it begins to boil at the rim, stir the potato starch mixture once again (the starch is prone to collect on the bottom), then begin to stir the soup broth. When it approaches a boil in earnest, add the starch and stir continuously.

A few cautions: If the broth is not sufficiently near the boiling point, it will become cloudy when the starch is added. Second, though you are seeking to thicken the broth, you are not after a condensed gelatin texture, but more of a thin gravy effect. The Japanese starch will continue to thicken after it has been added, so make adjustments as necessary. (After several attempts, you will know how you desire your broth and the timing necessary to achieve your desired result.) Last, the heat should be on high or medium-high (depending on the strength of the range) because as you add the starch, the temperature of the broth will drop considerably.

After you have added all of the starch, pour in the egg in a circular motion, beginning at the center and gradually working toward the rim. Knock the handle of the pot 3 or 4 times to ensure a thorough blending, as well as to prevent the starch from sticking on the bottom, then turn off the flame.

Reheat the noodles by putting then in a strainer and dipping them into the hot cooking water. Wring out the spinach and cut into 2-inch lengths. Place the noodles in individual bowls. Pour in the broth, then place the cut spinach and fish cakes on top. Garnish with a dab of ginger, finely sliced scallions, and *shiso*. Serve immediately.

## Chicken and Leek Soba

This is a variation of a dish which originally called for duck. Chicken has a lighter taste, is available the year around, and is much cheaper to obtain than duck. The aim in cooking the chicken is to maintain a suitably soft and moist texture.

**Serves 4**

1¼ lbs homemade soba noodles
   or
1 lb dried soba noodles
6½ cups hot broth
   or
10 Tbsps flavor base and 6 cups
   stock
½ lb young chicken
2 leeks
2 Tbsps soy sauce
2 Tbsps mirin
1 tsp sugar (optional)
Seven-spice pepper (shichimi)

Make the broth of your choice (pages 29–34).

Cut the chicken into thin, bite-sized pieces and the leeks into long, thin, diagonal slices. Fry together in a skillet with the soy sauce, *mirin*, and sugar over a high heat for 30 seconds.

Boil, wash, and reheat the noodles (page 26).

Place in a bowl, add the chicken and leeks, and cover with the steaming broth. Serve immediately. Season to taste with pepper.

## Curry Soba

The hot and spicy taste of curry also complements soba noodles very well. This is one of those dishes that is received equally well in the cold of winter as well as on a hot summer day. In winter it warms the body, while in the summertime its thick, spicy, hot broth has a cool, settling effect on the body. Some recipes call for pork, chicken, or shrimp to be added for additional flavor, but curry spice and juicy leeks by themselves produce a sufficiently satisfying dish and the combination is thus quite popular among vegetarians.

> 1¼ *lbs homemade soba noodles*
>    *or*
> 1 *lb dried soba noodles*
> 6½ *cups hot broth*
>    *or*
> 10 *Tbsps flavor base and 6 cups stock*
> 4 *tsps curry powder*
> 4 *Tbsps potato starch (katakuriko) or kuzu or 6 Tbsps cornstarch (or to taste)*
> 2 *leeks*
> 2 *scallions, finely sliced*

Make the broth of your choice (pages 29–34).

Combine the curry and starch with 6 Tbsps broth. Mix well. Chop the leeks in half lengthwise and then cut into bite-sized pieces so that they will cook easily.

Bring the broth to a boil and add the leeks. Return the broth to a boil, then slowly pour in the curry mixture, stirring constantly. When the broth is adequately thickened, and again comes to a boil, turn off the flame. The strength of the curry and the thickness of the soup is up to your own discretion, but generally a rich gravylike (but not lumpy) broth with a good, strong curry flavor is the most popular.

Boil, wash, and reheat the noodles (page 26).

Place the noodles in individual bowls. Pour or ladle the broth on top. The broth should amply cover the noodles. Garnish with sliced scallions and serve immediately.

## Flavored Soba Noodles                                *Gozen Soba*

Three hundred years ago, soba noodles appealed mainly to priests, temple patrons, country people, laborers, and the lower classes. Soba was cheap and quick to eat, light in calories, yet fortifying and satisfying.

Soba chefs knew they had a good thing. Eventually, they developed a pride in their trade that has carried right on down to the present. Like the sushi or tofu maker, they tried to upgrade their fare by coming up with a more "sophisticated" variation that would appeal to aristocrats, lords, and ultimately the shogun himself. The result was the simple but elegant variation which became known as soba that was fit "to be served before nobles," as the Japanese name implies.

Flavored Soba uses a highly refined, white buckwheat flour. The resulting noodle, with its light taste and texture as well as its appealing snow-white color, is said to have been just the ticket to awaken the upper classes' appreciation of buckwheat. And as its taste is very subtle, it is usually accompanied by only a small amount of broth.

In addition, because this flour is derived from the heart of the kernel it has comparatively little elasticity and hence must be kneaded together with boiling water and wheat flour.

One of the most famous of these flavored sobas is Green Tea Soba. It originated in Shizuoka, an area renowned for its high-quality green tea and the chosen retirement area of the shogun Tokugawa Ieyasu. The leaves of the tea plant are dried and turned into powder. Later, they are mixed into the white buckwheat flour, producing a sweet and aromatic noodle. Some chefs cover the noodles with hot water just before serving them to bring out their full fragrance.

Serves 4-6

5¼ cups white buckwheat flour
   (sarashina)* and 2¼ cups
   wheat flour
   or
4½ cups standard buckwheat
   flour and 3 cups wheat flour

3 cups water

1¾ cups dipping sauce
   or
7 Tbsps flavor base and 1¼
   cups stock

FLAVORING (choose one)

6 yuzu citrus (yellow)

6 oz black sesame seed (black)

6 oz parsley or powdered green
   tea (matcha) or shiso leaves
   (green)

Prepare the flavoring first.

YELLOW: Grate the yuzu to obtain the zest. Stop before you reach the bitter pith.

BLACK: Grind the sesame seeds with a mortar and pestle.

GREEN: Wash the parsley or shiso leaves well and then mince or whir in a food processor. The powdered tea can be used as is.

While bringing the water to a boil, combine the pure-white buckwheat flour and wheat flour in a mixing bowl. Make an open hole in the center of the flour, and pour the boiling water in all at once.

Stir the boiling water into the flour with long wooden spatulas or cooking chopsticks. For the first minute, just continue stirring in a circular motion. Have a helper fan the flour with a newspaper as you do this (or use an electric fan set on a low speed).

---

*This first combination of flours produces a white noodle if flavoring is omitted. The standard flour produces, of course, the typical brown soba noodle. When adding a flavor to the latter, the colors will be somewhat muted by this darker flour. In Japan, the pure-white sarashina flour is quite expensive and available only in 50-pound bags. I hope to be able to offer this flour to any reader wishing to try this gourmet style of soba (see the back of this book).

Continue stirring and kneading with your fingertips and palms, as for regular soba (pages 15–25), for at least 2 minutes.

Now add the flavoring agent directly into the buckwheat flour and mix for 1 minute. Finally, add the wheat flour and finish kneading.

Roll out and cut just as for standard soba.

Cook until the noodles are *al dente* (page 26).

## Soba Salad

This is a very popular dish to help ward off the summer heat, which may ruin even the heartiest of appetites. The key to this recipe is to prepare a good seasoning and to attain an appetizing balance of colors.

| | |
|---|---|
| 1¼ | *lbs homemade soba noodles* |
| | *or* |
| 1 | *lb dried soba noodles* |
| 1¼ | *cups chilled broth* |
| 12 | *stalks asparagus* |
| ¼ | *red onion* |
| 1 | *cucumber* |
| 2 | *tomatoes* |
| 4 | *leaves lettuce* |
| 1¼ | *lbs ham (optional)* |
| 4 | *tsps mayonnaise* |
| 4 | *tsps French dressing* |

**Serves 4**

Make the broth of your choice (pages 29–34) and chill (page 32).

Trim the asparagus and boil for 3 to 4 minutes over a high flame in lightly salted water. Remove from heat to a bowl of cold water.

Slice the onion. Wash and peel the cucumber (if necessary), then quarter lengthwise and cut into bite-sized chunks. Wash the lettuce and tear into small pieces. Slice each tomato into 8 wedges. Dice the ham. Cut the asparagus into 2-inch lengths.

Boil, wash, and drain the noodles (page 26).

Line individual bowls with the lettuce. Add the noodles and garnish with vegetables. Pour in the broth and add a dollop of mayonnaise and French dressing. Mix well before eating.

# Country Cooking

Just as many areas in Japan have long been famous for their production of high-quality buckwheat, many of the local areas have developed their own distinctive ways of making soba noodles that are likewise famous throughout the country. In fact, having ready access to good-quality buckwheat flour, the people of these areas grew up appreciating food made from the freshest flour.

Becoming intimate with buckwheat's true character, they naturally developed styles reflecting their understanding. Even today, these regional styles enjoy unfading popularity and are appreciated for presenting buckwheat's character in subtly different ways.

Many of these regional styles have found their way into the mainstream of soba cuisine, and so properly belong with the general noodle dishes of the preceding section. Two such dishes are Green Tea Soba (see Flavored Soba, page 66) and Soba Noodles with Grated Radish (page 54).

Of the four recipes introduced here, only Tsugaru Soba has inherited the name of its place of origin. Other types or variations include Izumo Soba (from Shimane Prefecture), Echizen Soba (Fukui Prefecture), Iya Soba (Tokushima Prefecture), Tsushima Soba (Nagasaki Prefecture), Tokosei Soba (Hyogo Prefecture), and Shirakawa Soba (Fukushima Prefecture). (Most or all of these are either variations on a standard soba recipe or call for the introduction of a favored local food.)

"Silk Cut" Soba takes its name not from a place but rather from the special cutting technique developed to accommodate 100-percent soba noodles. The knife slides across the well-kneaded dough, "shearing" it as kimono-maker of old sheared high-quality silk.

Of the remaining two recipes, one takes its name from its ingredients and the other from its container. Soba Noodles in a Miso Stew received its Japanese name from the smorgasbord-like variety of ingredients added to a miso soup base. Wanko Soba got its from the small bowls automatically replenished with yet another portion of noodles until the diner called a stop. This all-you-can-eat style originated in real soba country.

## Soba Noodles in a Miso Stew *Kenchin Soba (Ibaragi Prefecture)*

Ibaragi Prefecture lies to the north of Tokyo and is known for its tasty produce, such as carrots, burdock, and daikon radishes. This dish combines tender vegetables sauteed in sesame oil with soba and a miso broth for a hearty bowl of noodles said to have been eaten in earlier times by the famed samurai of Mito (a clan related to the Tokugawa) at New Year's to ensure strength and vigor.

Today, local residents turn to this stewlike soba dish for warmth and nourishment when they need to fend off the cold of winter. The blend of miso and broth is sure to satisfy Western palates as well, be they those of warriors or not.

1¼ lbs fresh noodles
    or
1 lb dried noodles
7 Tbsps flavor base
6 cups stock
½ block tofu
1 burdock root
1 carrot
2 oz bamboo shoots
4 dried shiitake mushrooms, softened (page 95)
6 leaves spinach
¼ lb chicken (optional)
2 Tbsps sesame or vegetable oil
4–5 Tbsps miso
Pinch salt
Dash saké

**Serves 4**

Cut the tofu into 6 or 8 pieces, wrap in cellophane, and freeze overnight. Thaw and squeeze out the moisture.

Combine the stock and flavor base.

Sliver the burdock and carrots and soak the burdock in water. Slice the bamboo shoots diagonally. Slice the mushrooms.

Parboil the spinach and place into a bowl of cold water (to maintain the color). Wring out and cut into 2-inch lengths.

Cut the chicken into small pieces, season well with salt and saké, and pan-fry in oil. In a separate pan, lightly saute the burdock and carrots.

Place the vegetables, chicken, and tofu in the broth and allow to boil for just a moment. Dissolve the miso in ½ cup of hot broth. Add to broth, stir well, and remove from heat.

Boil, wash, and reheat the noodles (page 26), then place in serving bowls. Cover with the broth and serve immediately.

VARIATION: Serve the hot broth as a dipping sauce with chilled noodles.

# Soy-Soba Noodles
*Tsugaru Soba (Aomori Prefecture)*

This style was very popular at the "nighthawk" soba carts in eighteenth- and nineteenth-century Tokyo. By substituting mashed soybeans for water during the all-important mixing process, the soba masters of old found that not only they could offer a new, flavorful noodle but they could keep the cooked noodles for as long as 3 or 4 days. (Standard noodles are prone to dry and turn sour within 12 to 24 hours, depending on the season.) The ability of this soy-soba noodle to maintain its freshness led to the nickname "illusion soba." That is, if properly wrapped and stored, the noodles look as fresh 3 or 4 days later as they do on the day they are made.

*4 oz soybeans*

*½ cup water*

*4 cups buckwheat flour*

*2 cups wheat flour*

**Serves 4**

DAY ONE

Soak the soybeans in ample water until they double in size. In warm summer weather this will take 10 to 12 hours. In winter, allow 24 hours.

Bring ½ cup of water to a boil and remove from heat. Add ¾ cup of buckwheat flour and mix following the recipe for Soba Dumpling (page 79).

Remove dough to a large bowl of cold water (use ice water in hot weather). Let sit for 24 hours.

DAY TWO

Rinse and wash the soybeans. Slowly grind with a mortar and pestle or whir in a food processor until you achieve a smooth, porridgelike consistency (add a small amount of water if necessary).

Drain the dumpling dough well and mix it together with the remaining buckwheat flour.

Now, adding only about one-third of the soybean puree at a time, mix together following the directions in Homemade Soba Noodles (page 15). No additional water is necessary.

Roll out the noodles and cut.

Set aside for least 5 hours in summer and overnight in winter until the noodles turn an amber or light brown and their fragrance is irresistible.

Cook as you would regular soba noodles (page 26). Serve immediately.

# Wanko Soba
*(Iwate Prefecture)*

In the Tohoku district of northern Japan, this soba has been served for several centuries. Today, travelers to the area never fail to sample this regional fare, perfect for hearty appetites.

The "spirit of *wanko*" (which means "small bowl") is akin to the all-you-can-eat buffets in the West. Traditionally, contests have been held to determine a local champion. A waiter or waitress stands behind each contestant, replacing the petite bowls of noodles as fast as they are emptied. A mouthwatering assortment of condiments—mushrooms, cooked greens, sashimi, shrimp, and so on—is served along with the noodles, and hungry contestants have been known to eat upward of 50 or 60 bowls of fresh soba pasta!

Wanko's legacy pervades the area. Even out-of-town customers who stop in at a local soba shop are asked—with a smile—if they would like to try to best the existing shop record.

In any case, this style of soba lends itself to picnics, parties, or any buffet-type affair—all the more so since soba and alcohol go well together.

The toppings below are only suggestions. Add to them or change the portions as you see fit. Other possible toppings may include cooked and chopped greens (such as spinach or asparagus), ground chicken, or cottage cheese and pineapple.

2½  *lbs fresh soba noodles*
    *or*
1½  *lbs dried soba noodles*
 2  *cups flavor base*
 6  *cups stock*
 1  *lb assorted seafood (cooked shrimp or white fish; sushi toppings such as tuna sashimi, shrimp, salmon roe, etc.)*
    *Dash saké (for salmon roe)*
    *Oil for deep-frying (for tempura)*
½  *lb cooked greens (spinach, asparagus, cabbage, etc.)*

**Serves 6–8**

CONDIMENTS
 8  *Tbsps sesame seeds*
 1  *cup sliced scallion*
 2  *cups grated daikon radish*
1–2  *sheets nori seaweed, toasted (page 94) and shredded*
    *Bonito flakes*

Combine flavor base and stock to make broth. Set aside to cool for about 2 hours or force-cool in a large bowl of ice water.

Roast the sesame seeds in a dry skillet until they begin to emit a nice nutlike fragrance. Do not allow them to pop. Remove them immediately from the pan. Serve whole or grind into a coarse powder.

To ensure their maximum freshness, prepare the daikon and onions just before serving. If prepared earlier, wrap tightly in plastic wrap.

Prepare the seafood. If you are using shrimp, boil them (seasoning to taste) or make tempura (page 55). Season salmon roe with a dash of saké. Deep-fry white fish and chop into bite-sized pieces. Last, coarsely chop tuna or other sashimi.

Chop cooked greens into bite-sized pieces.

Arrange each topping neatly in its own dish. Since there are a variety of toppings, try to use dishes of the same color and size. Place a folded white napkin under oily foods.

Cook the noodles and cool (page 26) just before you are ready to sit down at the table.

Serve the noodles at room temperature. Set out the noodles on a large platter and allow the diners to help themselves. Take a small portion of noodles and cover it with one or more toppings. Dip the noodles halfway into the chilled sauce. Season the dipping sauce with one or more condiments of your choice.

## "Silk Cut" Soba         *Tachi Soba (Fukushima Prefecture)*

There are three technical feats about this style that make it stand out from the rest. One is that the dough is made with 100-percent buckwheat flour. Second, boiling water is added to initiate the kneading process and then, after about 1 minute of kneading, cold water is introduced. Third, a unique cutting method is employed which closely resembles the cutting of silk for a kimono. The Japanese verb *tatsu* means to pull the cutting knife straight down and through the material. Hence, this style has become known as *Tachi Soba*. (It should not be confused, however, with *tachi-gui*, the "instant" variety of soba found at fast-food soba stands.)

One of its places of origin is recorded to be in the remote mountain village of Hinoemata in Fukushima Prefecture, where snow covers the ground half of the year. Buckwheat was one of the only crops that flourished, and other staples such as wheat and rice were simply not obtainable. As a result, the people developed this unique style, which allowed them to make 100-percent buckwheat noodles.

These noodle were accompanied by only the simplest of broths (again, due to limited local food sources), and when the supply of soy sauce ran out, homemade miso was used to liven up the soup. Fish from the cold mountain stream that divides Hinoemata in half were also used to make a broth. Fortunately, today there are more choices. Choose any of broths in this book or whip up a hearty broth of your own.

*3 cups fresh, high-quality
buckwheat flour (or use 2 cups
buckwheat flour and 1 cup
wheat flour)*

*2 scant cups water*

**Serves 8–10**

Add ¾ cup boiling water to the flour. Knead for 45 seconds to a minute and then add 1¼ cups cold water. Knead the dough thoroughly as in Homemade Soba Noodles (pages 15–25) and then divide it into 4 or 5 balls.

With a standard rolling pin, roll out each ball separately. While aiming to attain a nice circular shape, roll out until it reaches a thickness of ⅛ inch. Roll away from you, turning the dough like a steering wheel, with your hands at 10 and 2, after 3 or 4 rolls. Stack one piece on top of the other, lightly sprinkling with flour to prevent sticking.

Cut the stack in half and place one pile on the other. This helps somewhat to prevent the dough from tearing when you cut. (Do not fold the dough. It will crack and tear easily because it contains little or no wheat and hence lacks wheat's gluten to bind the dough.)

Now you are ready for the "silk cutting." Place your left hand on the dough with your left thumb near the cut edge. Align the knife with the edge so that your thumb is alongside the blade. Slide your hand 1 to 2 inches toward you, then cut into the dough with the knife, pulling it almost to your thumb. Repeat the slide-cut movement to cut a noodle ⅛ inch wide.

The left hand accompanies and actually leads the slicing motion of the knife. After a few times you will get a feel for the rhythm required and gradually surprise yourself at how straight you will be able to cut. Even if you can only approximate a shoelace-type shape, the noodles will have a special edge to them that is different from the edges of noodles obtained from the professional's big, thick knife, and is sure to surprise your family and friends. After a few attempts, the cutting becomes easier and easier.

Because this noodle is made from 100-percent buckwheat flour, it dries out easily and must be protected. When finished rolling and cutting, wrap in newspaper or plastic wrap and keep in a cool place to prevent drying if you are not going to immediately cook and serve the noodles. Noodles keep 2 or 3 days, depending on the weather.

Cook following the standard instructions (page 26), but treat more gently. If the noodles appear as if they may break apart during the cooking, place them in a wire strainer and lower it into slowly boiling water. Cook until done (1 minute), testing frequently. Serve immediately.

# Groat Cooking

Served as a principal food in several parts of Europe, this unpretentious food provides a nice alternative or addition to any breakfast, lunch, or dinner menu.

In Japan, it might be served up in a stew along with ingredients such as *shiitake* mushrooms, bamboo shoots, onions, chicken, and shrimp, or dressed with various kinds of sauces as part of the soba haute cuisine (*soba kaiseki*) course, or even in a miso sauce topping for a soba dumpling. In Russia, it was formerly eaten by the lower class and nobility alike. In fact, buttered groats was the favorite dish of the czar Peter the Great, and some said that he seldom supped on anything else.

## Kasha (Boiled Groats)

When cooking groats, remember that the cooking time will differ according to the amount of water, the variety of the groat, the season, and so on, but about 20 minutes is a good rule of thumb to go by.

Groats are usually boiled, but they are sometimes dry-roasted in a skillet first for added flavor. The boiling method here employs a little-by-little approach. That is, the cooking water is changed twice as soon as it comes to a boil. Only the third pot of cooking water is kept. In this way, the color of the groats becomes lighter, the taste subtler yet, and the tedious process of washing the groats over and over is eliminated. This method of preparation comes from soba haute cuisine. Whether to change the cooking water is left up to your discretion, as from a nutritional point of view it is debatable whether nutrition would be lost or not.

*2 cups groats*                                                    **Serves 4**

Roast the groats before boiling if desired. To do this, heat them in a dry skillet over a medium flame until they turn a golden brown and emit a nutlike fragrance. Stir often and do not allow them to scorch.

Wash the groats, put into a pot, and add water to cover. Bring the water to a boil over a medium-high flame.

Drain, return to the pot, add water to cover, and bring to a boil a second time.

Drain the groats and return to the pot a third time. Add 2¼ cups water, reduce heat to low and simmer for 15 to 20 minutes until the water has been absorbed.

Serve plain or seasoned to taste with butter, sour cream, or grated cheese.

## Groats Simmered in a Bonito Stock

2 cups groats
2½ cups bonito stock

**Serves 4**

Make the stock of your choice (pages 29–34).

Wash and rinse the groats thoroughly. Soak in the stock for 1 hour.

Bring the groats and stock to a boil and then simmer (loosely covered) over a very low heat until the groats become light and fluffy and all the liquid is absorbed (about 30 minutes).

## Buckwheat Groats and Brown Rice Mushi

Here is a prime example of complementary proteins and vitamins of separate foods boosting the overall protein value of a dish (as discussed in the Nutrition section).

1⅓ cups brown rice
⅔ cup buckwheat groats
3 cups water
4 fresh shiitake mushrooms, thinly sliced
½ lb chicken, sliced (optional)
½ carrot, finely chopped
6 oz bamboo shoots, finely sliced
1 block tofu, chopped into small cubes
4 Tbsps flavor base or 3 Tbsps soy sauce, 1 Tbsp mirin, and 1 tsp sugar

**Serves 4**

Wash the brown rice and buckwheat groats well and let sit for 2 to 3 hours.

Strain and bring to a boil in 3 cups water. Reduce to a simmer and cook (loosely covered) for 35 to 40 minutes.

After 25 minutes, layer in the remaining ingredients. Cover with the flavor base and allow to simmer and finish cooking. Serve in bowls.

## Groat Salad with Vinegar Dressing

1 cup buckwheat groats
8 small or 4 large shrimp
½ oz dry wakame seaweed
1 small cucumber
2 Tbsps light soy sauce

**Serves 4**

4 Tbsps rice vinegar

2 Tbsps mirin

2 Tbsps stock

1 oz walnuts, chopped

Cook the groats as you would for Kasha (page 75).

Clean the shrimp and remove the tails. Boil for 1 minute in lightly salted water.

Soak the *wakame* in water for 15 minutes. Rinse well and chop finely. Slice the cucumber into thin rounds.

Combine the soy sauce, *mirin*, vinegar, and stock.

Lightly toss the groats, shrimp, *wakame*, and cucumber. Cover with the dressing, sprinkle with the walnut, and serve.

## Soba Groat Zosui

*Zosui*

1 cup buckwheat groats

1 cup leftover rice

½ block tofu

4 leaves spinach, finely chopped

6 mushrooms, coarsely chopped

¼ lb ground chicken

¼ carrot, diced

4 cups hot soba stock (pages 29–34)

6 Tbsps flavor base or 4 Tbsps soy sauce, 1½ Tbsps mirin, and 2 tsps sugar

**Serves 4**

Wash the groats well and soak in water for about an hour.

Heat up the stock and add the rice and groats when it reaches a boil.

Add the remaining ingredients, lower the flame slightly, and pour in the flavor base. Simmer for 5 to 7 minutes. Serve piping hot in soup bowls.

## Groat and Okara Mélange

⅓ cup buckwheat groats

3–4 Tbsps vegetable oil

½ carrot, diced

2 fresh shiitake *or other mushrooms, thinly sliced*

8 green beans, slivered

7 oz okara

3 Tbsps light soy sauce

3. Tbsps sugar

3 Tbsps mirin

½ cup hot soba stock (pages 29–34)

**Serves 4**

Soak the groats in water for 2 hours. When the groats become fluffy, drain off the remaining water.

Heat oil in a pan and stir-fry the vegetables and groats for a few minutes.

Add the *okara*, soy sauce, sugar, and *mirin* and continue stirring for 3 to 4 minutes until the *okara* emits a nutlike fragrance.

Finally, add the stock and cook over a medium flame until the liquid is absorbed (about 5 minutes). Serve in a fluffy mound garnished with a few slivers of green beans.

## Seafood Groat Patties

2 cups buckwheat groats

5 cups soba stock (pages 29–34)

8 eggs

¼ lb fish, diced

6 clams, diced

1 onion, diced

Garlic to taste

**Serves 4**

First, cook the groats in the stock following the recipe on page 76. Drain off excess liquid.

Beat the eggs. Mix the fish, clams, onions, and garlic together in bowl and then combine with the egg.

Finally, mix in the very soft and well-cooked groats. Form into thin patties and fry in a skillet until cooked through (about 5 minutes).

## Groat and Mountain Yam Fry

⅓ cup buckwheat groats

Rice vinegar (for soaking yam)

7 oz mountain yam (yama imo)

1½ cups bonito stock (pages 29–34)

Pinch sugar

Pinch salt

3 Tbsps potato starch (katakuriko) or cornstarch

Oil for deep-frying

**Serves 4**

Wash the groats well and parboil in 1 cup water. Allow to cool.

Peel the yam and soak in vinegar water (5 parts water to 1 part vinegar) for about 5 minutes. Cut into rounds. Bring the stock, sugar, and salt to a boil, add the yams, and simmer until soft (3 to 5 minutes).

Grind the yam and stock with a mortar and pestle. Pour this thickened mixture into the bowl of cooked groats and mix well.

Form into ping-pong-sized balls. Roll in starch.

Preheat the oil. Deep-fry balls until they float and turn a golden brown.

# Variations and Desserts

## Soba Dumpling                                    *Soba Gaki*

Though of plain appearance, this dumpling provides the maximum benefits of buckwheat's nutritional elements, notably vitamin B. Furthermore, since all of the water used in the recipe is combined with the flour during the cooking process (no other water or cooking is necessary), practically all of buckwheat's water-soluble elements remain in the dumpling itself. (The professional, however, boils the finished dumpling one more time after mixing to create a softer, more delicate texture.)

There are two basic methods of making buckwheat dumplings: in a pot over a flame or in a bowl. The pot method utilizes a high flame during the beating process to heat the dough, while the bowl style takes the opposite approach of pouring boiling water into the bowl of flour and beating without the benefit of any additional heat. In the pot method, the buckwheat flour can either be combined with cold water before beating over a flame (a good technique for beginners to use), or after you gain more confidence, the flour can be mixed with rapidly boiling water (the professional method).

The pot style has a higher success rate as the buckwheat flour has virtually no choice but to gelatinize with continuous heating and pounding. Plus, you can adjust the flame as you go along. Since these factors play no role in the bowl method, be sure to use rapidly boiling water.

Furthermore, there is a delicate difference between immersing flour (buckwheat or any other kind) into a pot of boiling water and pouring boiling water into a bowl of flour. The pot style provides a smoother, shinier, and more consistent texture, while it is claimed that the fragrance of the dumpling obtained by the bowl method is superior. That is, buckwheat's delicate and treasured fragrance has no chance to escape since the flour is not heated or cooked.

This last point provides a hint that applies to whichever method is employed. That is, while working to develop buckwheat's viscosity, you must also move quickly so as to prevent any loss of its delicate fragrance.

The pot method is introduced in detail below. Once you become familiar with the way buckwheat behaves under heat you will be able go on to the professional method, or if you prefer you can make the dumpling in a bowl simply by transferring the boiling water to a large mixing bowl.

Serves 4

> 4½ cups buckwheat flour
> 2⅓ cups water*
> 1¾ cups broth
> or
> 7 Tbsps flavor base and 1¼ cups stock
> Nori seaweed, toasted and shredded (page 94)
> Wasabi horseradish
> 1 stalk scallion, finely sliced

Make the broth of your choice (pages 29–34).

Divide both the flour and water in half. Combine 1 portion of water with 1 portion of flour. Mix well.

With the flame up high, use a pestle (4 to 5 chopsticks clenched in one fist, a wooden spoon, or even a spatula in emergencies) to beat the flour into the water. With quick, rhythmical, circular strokes, begin to combine the flour and the water. Keep the wrist loose. At this initial stage, the flour and water will not form a dough easily, but will form small, marble-sized pebbles. (Interestingly, this is exactly what happens during the initial stages of soba noodle making: *it takes time for the flour to bind together into one large ball of dough.*)

As you continue beating rhythmically, stroke by stroke, the dough will begin to form. Continue to beat in a circular motion and gather all of the dough into a single ball against the side of the pan closest you. When this is achieved, remove from the heat. (The pros, who are aiming for the highest degree of sweetness, continue beating over a medium-high flame until they can smell a sweet, scorching fragrance, and the surface of the dough closest to the heat turns a light brown similar to that of crepes.)

Lay a slightly moist cloth or towel on top of the counter. Place the pot on the towel and continue beating until you achieve a smooth, gelatinized texture. (Although it contains no gluten, buckwheat does have a large amount of high-quality starch which becomes extremely sticky and viscous when mixed with hot water.) Keep in mind that the whole beating process takes only 40 to 60 seconds and that the movement of the pestle will meet with increasing resistance as the gelatinization occurs.

As the dough forms and the pestle becomes more difficult to wield, a pleasant "puckering" sound will become audible. This is your assurance that you

---

*According to the time of year and condition of the flour, the amount of water required can vary by as much as 20 percent. Freshly harvested flour needs less water than flour that has been sitting on the shelf. Furthermore, the quality of the grind will also influence the moisture content of the flour.

The key to success, then, in almost all of the buckwheat recipes lies in adding the water quickly but little by little. After 5 or 10 attempts, you will develop a good intuitive sense as to how much water to add.

have performed the job well. There should be a distinct difference in the texture of the dough before and after you hear this sound. Continue beating for another 5 seconds to achieve a firm dough.

Switching from the pestle to a flat wooden spoon or rice paddle (in an emergency any flat-surfaced utensil will do), press the finished soba dumpling into a nicely compact shape against the side of the pot. Dip the paddle in hot water 2 or 3 times during this final stage to obtain a smoother and shinier surface. Divide into 2 balls. Decorate the tops with a simple design. (Professionals use the edge of their wooden paddle to incise a leaf pattern.)

Repeat the process with the remaining flour and water.

Serve with heated or chilled broth. Garnish with the nori, *wasabi*, and scallion.

## Steamed Soba Dumpling with Shrimp and Mountain Yam

   3 *cups buckwheat flour*
1½ *cups dipping sauce*
   *or*
   ¼ *cup flavor base and 1¼ cups cold stock*
1¼ *cups hot stock*
   1 *avocado*
   5 *oz shrimp*
   5 *oz mountain yam (yama imo)*

**Serves 4**

Make the dipping sauce and stock of your choice (pages 29–34) and let cool.

Scoop out the fruit of the avocado and grind in a mortar. Stir in the dipping sauce and blend into a creamy sauce.

Shell and devein the shrimp. With the dull back side of a heavy cooking knife, beat the shrimp into a pulp.

Peel the yam. Grate into a mortar. Add shrimp and 1 Tbsp of stock. Grind with a pestle until it becomes smooth.

Combine this mixture with the buckwheat flour and half of the stock. Knead the dough following the directions for the Soba Dumpling (page 79). Add broth as necessary. Form into small patties.

Cook the dumplings in a preheated steamer for 4 to 5 minutes, or until little bubble pockets form like beads on the outside. Serve with the avocado dipping sauce.

VARIATION: Substitute walnut, *shiso,* and egg yolks for the yam. Place 1 oz walnuts, ⅔ oz *shiso* leaves, and 2 egg yolks in a food processor or blender. Whip well and then combine with flour and stock.

## Broiled Soba Dumpling with Miso Sauce

These savory miso-covered dumplings are best eaten "hot off the grill." The fragrant *yuzu* peel (which is also used in Korean and Chinese cooking) imparts a unique zestiness to the miso sauce, but if it is not readily available lemon or lime may be substituted.

4½ cups buckwheat flour

2¼ cups water

3–4 Tbsps sweet white miso

1 Tbsp grated *yuzu* zest (or lime or lemon zest)

1 tsp sugar or 1 Tbsp amazake

2 tsps basil

Skewers (optional)

Make the soba dumplings (page 79) and shape into hamburger-sized patties.

Make the miso sauce by mixing the miso with a little lukewarm water. Add the grated *yuzu* and mix well, then add the sugar.

Pierce with skewers. Hold over a medium-low flame and turn over and over to lightly scorch both sides (or set the patties on a tray and place in a broiler).

Brush with a liberal coating of miso sauce, sprinkle with basil to taste, and pass over a flame (or broil) for about 30 to 40 seconds. Serve immediately.

## Soba-Sesame Tofu

1½ cups buckwheat flour (dark flour is best)

3 oz sesame butter or tahini

1½ oz kuzu *starch*

2 cups boiling water

1 scallion, finely sliced

Soy sauce

Wasabi *horseradish*

Dissolve the starch in a few tablespoons of cold water and allow it to sit for a moment. Stir well until the starch is completely dissolved. Run your fingertips along the bottom to make sure there are no hard clumps. (To obtain a softer texture, just decrease the amount of *kuzu*.)

Put the sesame butter into a pan and stir in one-fifth of the dissolved starch. Heat over a medium flame. Slowly add the remaining starch, stirring constantly for 2 to 3 minutes. Remove from the stove.

In a separate bowl, add the boiling water to the buckwheat flour. Whip with an eggbeater for about 5 minutes. (It is important to obtain a completely smooth, runny texture.) Return the *kuzu* mixture to the stove, turn the heat to medium, and pour in the buckwheat flour mixture while stirring continuously for 3 minutes.

Turn off the heat and pour the mixture into a pie or bread pan and refrigerate for 5 to 6 hours.

Before serving garnish with scallion, soy sauce, and *wasabi*. The recommended ingredients should produce a fairly firm and grainy tofu texture.

# Soba Sushi Roll

The thought of making sushi with soba noodles instead of rice always seems to raise eyebrows. Part of the reason is that rice is so closely associated with sushi. Moreover, people can't imagine how the long, slender noodles could possibly be tightly rolled into the required form. Yet once they get the hang of it, the idea that sushi belongs exclusively to the domain of rice quickly changes.

There are four key points to making good Soba Sushi:

1. Undercook the noodles slightly, cutting the cooking time by 10 to 15 seconds. (Aim: To produce a noodle that is cooked sufficiently, but just shy of its full elasticity.)

2. Wash and rinse the noodles thoroughly in cold water, or ice water in summer. (Aim: To firm up the noodle and keep it fresh. Later, this will provide the sushi with a nice chewy quality.)

3. Thoroughly drain the water from the noodles. (Aim: To prevent the noodles from becoming soggy.)

4. Work as quickly as possible. (Aim: To ensure the above three conditions.)

Just as with sushi rice, the soba noodles can be seasoned with rice vinegar, broth, or other flavoring agents. This recipe, however, will introduce a simple, unseasoned sushi.

| | |
|---|---|
| 2¼ | lbs cooked soba noodles |
| 8 | sheets nori seaweed |
| 5–6 | fresh shiitake or other mushrooms |
| 3 | oz bamboo shoots |
| 6 | Tbsps soy sauce |
| 2 | Tbsps mirin |
| 2 | tsps sugar |
| 3 | oz tuna |
| ¼ | cup finely sliced scallions |
| 4 | eggs |
| 2 | tsps sugar |
| ¼ | cup hot soba broth (pages 29–34), cooled |
| ⅔ | oz shiso leaves |
| 1½ | oz cucumber |
| 3 | oz cod roe (tarako) or any sashimi |
| 3 | oz salmon roe (ikura), sprinkled with dash saké |
| | Soy sauce |

**Yields 8 rolls**

Wasabi *horseradish*
*Bamboo rolling mat*
*Cheesecloth*

PREPARATION
Trim the width of the nori by 1 inch with a scissors.

Wash the mushrooms and bamboo, then slice very thinly. Combine each vegetable in its own pot with 3 Tbsps soy sauce, 1 Tbsp *mirin*, 1 tsp sugar, and enough water to cover. Bring to a boil, then simmer, loosely covered, until all of the liquid is absorbed (about 30 minutes).

Mix the tuna and scallions, then beat together with the dull side of a heavy knife.

Beat the eggs, cooled broth, and 2 tsps sugar together and cook as in "Rosy-Cheeked" Soba (page 60). Remove from the pan and set on a plate to cool. Repeat with the rest of the mixture. Cut each batch lengthwise into 3- or 4½-inch-wide strips.

Cut the *shiso* leaves into thin, ⅛-inch-wide strips.

Wash the cucumber and slice it and the sashimi into long, slender strips.

Cook the noodles (page 26), keeping the four key points in mind. Wash them in cold water as soon as they are done.

You cannot relax yet. If the noodles are left sitting in the rinsing bowl too long, they will absorb too much water before you know it. Therefore, the next step is to quickly shift the washed noodles to a large, dry strainer (or plate covered with cheesecloth). To prevent clumps or improper drying, the noodles should be spread around the edges of the strainer 4 to 5 strands at a time. Since the sides of the strainer slope inward, the water will naturally be inclined to flow in that direction, away from the noodles.

Allow to sit for 4 to 5 minutes. Fan with a newspaper. (Although this recipe introduces plain Soba Sushi, you could add vinegar to the process at this point, if so desired.)

Remove the noodles to a second dry strainer (or plate with cheesecloth) and allow to dry for an additional 4 to 5 minutes, fanning occasionally.

MAKING THE SUSHI ROLLS
Place a piece of cellophane over the bamboo rolling mat and on top of that place 1 sheet of nori. Spread out 20 to 25 noodles on the nori, leaving a 1-inch strip of nori uncovered at both the near and far ends.

Next place a long strip of egg in the middle of the noodles. On top of that, a few strips of *shiso*. To ensure that the egg and *shiso* stay in place, cover with another small mound of about 5 or 6 noodles.

Take hold of the end of the bamboo roller closest to you, and in one decisive motion, fold over to the point just past the furthest edge of the egg and *shiso*. Press down gently and hold for 3 seconds. Then with "the feeling of walking lightly with your fingers," roll forward until you reach the uncovered strip of nori at the far end. Again push down and hold. Finally, roll forward to cover the last bit of nori and again press and hold. With practice you should be able to make a clean, firm, and beautifully shaped roll. If you succeed the first time, consider opening your own restaurant. You have talent.

Proceed to wrap the remaining ingredients in the following combinations: mushroom with bamboo shoot, cucumber with cod roe (or sashimi), and salmon roe alone (to top sushi after it has been cut). (By the way, the combinations of stuffing for Soba Sushi are limitless. Anything that you can make into a soft yet firm shape will work well.)

Since the rolls should be cut just before serving, keep them wrapped in the cellophane and put in a cool place (but not in the refrigerator). When ready to cut, unwrap and place a damp cloth close by. Wipe both sides of a sharp knife on the cloth and cut a 1½-inch piece off in one smooth, continuous motion. Once you begin the slicing motion, do not stop until you have cut completely through the roll. Clean the knife on the cloth and make a second cut. Repeat until you have cut all the rolls.

NOTE: To make individual pieces of soba sushi with standard sushi toppings such as shrimp or squid (see color plate), simply press the noodles into a long block with a rolling mat lined with plastic wrap, cut into 2-inch lengths, and cover with the topping of your choice.

## Soba Pasty

This recipe allows you to show your creativity. The buckwheat dough can be stuffed with either sweet foods such as homemade pie or fruit filling, or sandwich-type fare such as hamburger, meat, cheese, or vegetables. Choose either of the fillings below or try one of your own.

4 cups buckwheat flour
2¼ cups boiling water

**Serves 4**

FILLINGS
1½ oz natto
4 tsps ground sesame seed
½ lb pickled vegetables (tsukemono) or parboiled spinach
or
½ lb fresh berries, peaches, or any other soft fruit
4 Tbsps sugar

Chop the *natto* as you would for *Natto* Soba (page 59). Mince the pickled vegetables or spinach (drain well first). Sprinkle with the sesame and mash together with the dull side of a knife. Season with soy sauce.

Chop the fruit: Parboil and drain well.

Combine the dough and water as in Soba Dumpling (page 79).

Divide the dough into 4 portions. Knead one of the balls separately in the mixing bowl about 10 times, take it out of the bowl, and knead with both hands to re-form into a ball. Keep a bowl of cold water on hand to moisten your hands as necessary.

Holding a ball of dough in the palm of the left hand, make a hole in the center of the ball with the index finger of your right hand. Rotate the ball, gradually widening the hole with your middle, index, and fourth fingers until you have formed the dough into a cup about the size of a half of a grapefruit. Use your fingers and finally a fist to shape the dough.

Pack in a tablespoon of filling at a time and gently press it down. Stop ½ inch shy of the rim. For the fruit filling spoon 1 Tbsp sugar into each cup.

Still holding the cup in the left palm, turn it around and around, gradually pinching the edges toward the center to close off the opening. Moisten your hands as often as necessary.

Steam or bake until small bubbles start to form on the surface. Serve immediately.

## Soba Crepe

These crepes have been a traditional dish in France for centuries. A French restaurant in Tokyo, where I helped out for two weeks, made soba crepes for the dinner menu. Choose one of the three fillings below or stuff the crepes with a dinner or dessert filling of your own.

1 cup buckwheat flour

½ tsp salt

1 egg

1½ cups water

Zest from 2 lemons, diced

Butter

**Makes 4 crepes**

FILLINGS (choose one)

¼ lb chicken

½ cup hot soba broth (pages 29–34)

1 tsp yuzu or lemon zest

4 tsps mustard
or

16 strips bacon

4 oz cheese

4 eggs
or

1 bundle asparagus

3 oz mushrooms

1⅓ cups milk

⅔ cup cream

¼ cup wheat flour

1 tsp oregano

2 tsps salt

Prepare the filling of your choice.

CHICKEN: Slice the chicken into 8 thin pieces, spread out 4 pieces each on a piece of tinfoil, fold up all the sides to make a tray, and pour in ¼ cup of hot broth. Sprinkle on the *yuzu* zest, fold up the foil, and put in a pot. Turn the flame up high and boil for 1 minute. Take out and cut each piece in half.

BACON: Fry the bacon and grate the cheese.

VEGETABLE: Boil the asparagus and mushrooms for 1 minute. Slice the mushrooms. Bring the milk, cream, wheat flour, oregano, and salt to a boil, then add the asparagus and mushrooms and simmer for 20 minutes.

Put the buckwheat flour and salt in a bowl and mix well. In a separate bowl, combine the lemon zest, water, and egg and beat well. Add to the flour and beat the mixture until it becomes even and creamy. Put into a bowl, cover with plastic wrap, and place in the refrigerator for at least an hour. (Professionals let it sit overnight.)

To cook the crepe, coat a saucepan with ample butter. (Try to use a pan that has been broken in, in order to avoid sticking.) Melt the butter over a high flame and pour off the excess.

Lower the heat to medium-low, then add another dab of butter and melt. Ladle in some batter. It should sizzle softly. Spread the batter by tilting the pan.

Fry the crepe until the batter just sets, then flip over. Add the fillings in layers. For the bacon, first spread a layer of cheese, then the bacon, and finally crack open an egg on top. For the chicken, spread the mustard first, the lettuce second, and the chicken third. For the vegetables, ladle some of the thickened sauce directly onto the crepe, then add the asparagus and mushroom.

As soon as the fillings have been added fold up the crepe. Fold up the top and bottom, then fold in the sides. Make sure the crepe covers the fillings completely, so that the crepe will seal. Cook until the crepe turns a light brown, then flip over and finish cooking.

Cover with melted butter or a sauce of your choice and serve immediately.

# Deep-fried Cinnamon Soba Dumpling with Tartar Sauce

4½ cups buckwheat flour

⅓ cup raisins, chopped

2 Tbsps ground cinnamon

1 tsp salt

2⅓ cups hot soba broth (pages 29–34)

Oil for deep-frying

Tartar sauce

Serves 4

Combine the raisins, cinnamon, and salt with the buckwheat flour.

Bring half of the broth to a boil, mix in half of the flour mixture, and beat into a dough following the standard Soba Dumpling method (page 79). Form into thin hamburger-shaped patties.

Preheat the oil to a low deep-frying temperature (300°–330°F). Deep-fry the dumplings until they float (about 1 minute).

Cover with Tartar sauce and serve immediately.

# Sweet Soba "Marshmallow" Dumplings     Soba Dango

As this recipe calls for a seemingly preposterous amount of sugar, it will probably be rejected by the editor, or cause surprise among the health-food crowd. But the fact of the matter is that without using this amount, it is impossible to attain the soft, marshmallowlike fluffiness that makes this dish so popular. In addition, most shops add sugar to the roasted soybean flour which traditionally coats this popular dessert. It must be taken into account that this kind of sweet extravaganza is partaken of only on special occasions and is certainly not everyday fare. If eaten with this forgiving attitude, you will be surprised at how pleasant, and mild, it actually tastes.

**Serves 4**

1 cup buckwheat flour

1½ cups water plus ¾ cup sugar
  (Method A)
  or
¾ cup water and ¾ cup
  amazake (Method B)

½ cup sifted soy flour

½ cup sugar

Choose one of the following methods.

METHOD A: Bring the water to a boil, then add the sugar and stir until it dissolves. Allow it to cool for about 1 minute, or place the whole pan in a larger pan of cold water and stir for about 20 to 30 seconds. Add the buckwheat flour and stir very gently with a wooden spoon 5 or 6 times.

METHOD B: Whip the amazake in a blender for 10 seconds, then combine with the buckwheat flour and water.

Heat the mixture over a high flame and mix to make a dough in the same manner as in Soba Dumpling (page 79). If you have achieved the right consistency, you should be able to pull out the dough in one lump.

Moisten your hands in a bowl of cold water, then roughly break the dough into 20 to 24 bite-sized pieces. Rewet your hands as necessary. Roll each ball between your palms until smooth and round. Work as quickly as possible, as the dough will harden within several minutes. Combine the soy flour and sugar. Roll in the soy flour and serve immediately.

## Soba Butter Cookies

Butter cookies have been popular in France for centuries. Their popularity stems from their two contrasting textures: a light, crispy crust and a soft, mildly sweet inside.

This variation on the favored French standard calls for buckwheat flour and features buckwheat's grainy quality. To allow the adhesiveness of the buckwheat flour to develop fully it is important to "put air" into the mixture by tossing it over and over.

**Yields 2 dozen**

2 cups buckwheat flour

4 oz butter (1 cube)

6½ Tbsps sugar

  Pinch salt

4 tsps vanilla

6 egg yolks

⅔ oz cocoa powder

Place the buckwheat flour and softened butter into a bowl and mix together, tossing well.

Let the "grains" fall through your fingertips as you rub your hands together in a light and quick manner. Continue mixing until the overall texture becomes damp and powderlike.

Mix the sugar and salt in another bowl. Add the egg yolks and vanilla, then beat rapidly with an eggbeater in a circular motion until the mixture becomes white and creamy.

Combine the egg mixture with the flour and butter. Mix lightly.

After the whole is well blended, form the flour into a dough.

Remove the dough to a cutting board and knead into a ball. Divide the dough into two portions. Add the cocoa to one portion and mix until dough turns a deep brown.

Roll both portions of dough into cylinders 1½ inches in diameter. Wrap tightly in plastic wrap and refrigerate for at least an hour.

Retrieve the cylinders from the refrigerator. Cut into ⅛-inch-thick slices and place on a greased baking pan. Bake in a preheated oven (340°F) for 7 to 10 minutes or until the edges brown.

## Soba Crunch

When buckwheat flour is deep-fried it becomes crispy and makes an ideal snack food. The finished sticks may be coated with syrup, as suggested below, or in honey.

| | |
|---|---|
| 1½ cups buckwheat flour | **Yields 4 dozen** |
| 1⅔ tsps baking powder | |
| 4 eggs, lightly beaten | |
| Vegetable oil for deep-frying | |
| 3½ oz brown or black sugar | |
| ¼ cup water | |

Mix the flour and baking powder together in a bowl. Make a well in the center of the flour and add the eggs. Knead the mixture until it becomes smooth and satiny. Form into a ball and allow it to rise for at least 1½ hours. Knead well once more.

Roll out dough into ropes about ¼ inch in diameter, then cut into 5-inch lengths.

Preheat the oil and deep-fry the sticks until they are lightly fried.

To make the syrup, combine the sugar with ¼ cup water in a saucepan over a medium heat and stir well until the liquid thickens. Coat deep-fried sticks well. Serve with finger bowl or damp cloth.

## Soba Mochi Squares                                    *Hatto*

This is another Hinoemata specialty. Buckwheat flour combined with sweet rice gruel is boiled and then topped with a blend of roasted sesame, cinnamon, and sugar. Served steaming hot, these soft-textured squares have just the right amount of oil and substance to make an excellent afternoon snack.

2 cups buckwheat flour

1 cup sweet rice (mochi-gome)

¼ cup sesame seeds

2 Tbsps sugar

1 tsp salt

2 tsps cinnamon

Wash the sweet rice and soak in water to cover for 6 to 8 hours or overnight. Drain well and put in a pan together with 3 cups water. Bring to a boil, cover loosely, and simmer for 45 minutes.

Combine the sesame seeds, sugar, salt, and cinnamon and grind in a mortar and pestle.

Knead the thin sweet-rice gruel into the buckwheat flour. When all of the liquid is absorbed, add ½ to 1 cup water and knead until you have soft, spongelike dough.

Roll out into a rectangular shape about ¼ inch thick and cut into 2-inch squares. (If placed in plastic wrap and refrigerated at this point, the uncooked dough will keep for a week.)

Bring ample water to a rapid boil. Place the squares in the boiling water. When they float to the surface, scoop them out.

Coat the boiled squares well with the crushed sesame mix. Serve immediately and eat while they are still hot.

## Saké-seasoned Soba Patties

4½ cups buckwheat flour

2⅓ cups saké

Bring half of the saké to a boil, then combine over heat with half of the flour as you would for Soba Dumpling (page 79). Repeat with remaining flour and saké.

For into patties and fry lightly in oil until golden brown on both sides. Serve immediately.

# Ingredients

Recently, Japanese food has jumped into the position of the sixth most popular ethnic cuisine in the United States. In the last ten years there has been a tremendous rise in the number of establishments serving Japanese fare. It seems that the more widely it is experienced and understood, the greater its appeal. The Japanese words *assari* and *sappari*, often used to describe feelings about food, give us a clue as to why this cuisine is finding such broad acceptance. *Assari* refers to a taste that is light and subtle, while *sappari* expresses one's feeling that the food is amply satisfying and refreshing.

The significance of these words goes a step further. In relation to cooking, they imply that a balance must be struck between rich and light ingredients. *Sappari* encourages us to think of the word "delicious" as entailing not only the initial burst of flavor but also the aftertaste or the way we feel hours after we have left the table.

The ingredients used in soba cuisine offer a whole new range of these *assari* and *sappari* foods to enjoy. With time you will be able to use these ingredients, perhaps insignificant when served individually, in combinations that will open up subtle new variations of taste and texture.

**Bonito flakes (*katsuo-bushi*):** An essential ingredient of the soba master's stock, bonito flakes are shaven from rock-hard pieces of dried bonito, which are either dried and fermented over a 4-month period or dried, rewashed, and then baked for about 7 to 8 minutes at high temperatures and immediately put through a shredder.

Nowadays, with increasing demand for natural and whole foods, the blocks of bonito are becoming more and more readily available in the West. The very best bonito stock is still made from freshly shaved flakes, which requires a special hand slicer. Freshly shaved chips have an exquisite taste which makes them good garnishes for almost any of the noodle dishes.

When buying flakes, look for those that are neatly shaved, are light in color, and have a nice, baconlike aroma. Once opened, they will keep for about 3 weeks if packed in cellophane and stored in the refrigerator.

**Burdock (*gobo*):** These roots are harvested from May to February. Good-quality roots are firm and straight, with unblemished skin. The best are without the hole in the center that forms when roots get thick. The skin is the best part of the root, so do not scrape it off but rather scrub with a stiff brush to clean it. In addition, in Japan, the leaves are dried, ground, and then added to the buckwheat flour during soba-making, giving a unique viscous quality to the noodles.

Burdock turns dark very quickly after being cut. To avoid discoloration, put the cut burdock into water, preferably with a touch of vinegar in it, as soon as possible.

**Daikon radish:** This long, white, stout Japanese radish abounds in vitamin C as well as digestive enzymes. Thus it is cherished for its ability to aid in digestion, especially of foods cooked in oil, like tempura. When cooked and seasoned with the soba broth, the sweetness of this radish comes through. But its main use is as a garnish for the chilled noodles. When grated, it tastes wonderfully hot and refreshing. Connoisseurs prefer it as hot as possible.

When used as a garnish, a radish which is not too watery and has a hot, spicy taste is preferable.

Whereas *wasabi* horseradish is grated from the head to the tip, daikon radish is ground from its tip (which is its hottest point) to the top. As you proceed upward, the daikon becomes more watery and the taste less spicy.

Once it has been grated, the freshness of this root evaporates quickly. It is essential, therefore, to keep it refrigerated in an airtight container once grated. Although only the most conscientious of restaurants will take the trouble to do so, when serving daikon at home, try to grate it just prior to serving.

**Daikon sprouts:** Large sprouts, used in salads and as a topping on oily dishes.

**Fish cakes (kamaboko):** *Kamaboko* is often used as an appetizer, and as such is a standard part of the *nuki* repertoire at high-class soba establishments (see The Soba Dining Experience). Served with a small dish of soy sauce and freshly grated *wasabi* horseradish, it is the Oriental version of gefilte fish.

Because the cakes can be sliced like salami and eaten "right from the stick," they are used to represent the cheeks in "Rosy-Cheeked" Soba. Or they can be simmered in water and eaten as a light snack with cheese and crackers, spread with yellow mustard, or cooked longer and allowed to become soft, as in an *oden* stew.

**Flour:** Choose your flour carefully. Look for the freshest possible flour and choose the product with the least amount of dark brown specks of ground hull, which gives the flour its slightly bitter taste. Ideally you want flour that has been hulled before the grinding. Japanese millers, as well as some European makers, do this and as a result produce a better flour.

If you are able to obtain Japanese flour, it is available in as many as seven different grades, ranging from the pure white *sarashina* flour, treasured for its high percentage of pure starch, through the yellowish green of the middle grades, to the dark chocolate brown of the protein-rich aleuron layer (see Part I). Since, under even optimum conditions, only 25 percent of the total yield is *sarashina* flour, it is the most costly, at $3 to $4 a pound wholesale. Used as a base in the Flavored Soba Noodles, it is indeed a delicacy item with a price. The yellowish green flour (*seiro*) accounts for roughly 35 percent of the yield, and sells for somewhat less. The chocolate-brown flour (*inakako*) constitutes about 35 percent. The remaining three basic flour types can be combined in any number of ways, and an endless variety of soba noodles can be produced.

***Konbu* kelp:** Used for its somewhat gelatinizing effect, *konbu* has flat, broad, thick leaves. Brownish black kelp liberally covered with a fine, white powder is a sign of quality. Lightly wipe the surface of the kelp with a damp cloth before using it. Store it in an airtight container.

There are a number of processed *konbu* varieties, such as *tororo-konbu*, which also work very well as a quick and tasty supplement for any soba dish requiring a hot broth. Ready-made *konbu*-stock products, often referred to as *konbu dashi*, are also available.

**Mirin:** *Mirin* is made from extracting the liquid from steamed and fermented sweet rice. Use this smooth-textured sweetener to add depth, taste, and fragrance to any dish. Discover how it works to not only sweeten food but also to add depth to the other ingredients by subtly blending into them.

After going through the period of fermentation, *mirin* acquires a slight percentage of alcohol. Yet, this alcohol content is said to react with the protein in fish and meat, ensuring that it will not break apart so easily while shortening cooking time by bringing out the flavor more quickly.

Furthermore, when *mirin* is combined with soy sauce or miso and put over a flame, the sweetness of the *mirin* and the amino acids within the soy sauce react to the heat, improving the flavor, glossiness, and color of the mixture.

Sometimes, before combining it with other ingredients, *mirin* is placed over a flame by itself and removed just before it reaches the boiling point. In addition to allowing its slight alcohol content to evaporate, this procedure also activates the sweetener and amino acids in the *mirin*, deepening its fragrance while mellowing its flavor even further.

Once bottled, the glucose and amino acids in the *mirin* will undergo a chemical reaction if exposed to direct sunlight, and in addition its color will change to a dark brown. Therefore, store in a cool, dark place.

**Miso:** Before the turn of the century, soy sauce was at times a luxury item which, in many a farming village, like Hinoemata (see "Silk Cut" Soba), was simply not available. Throughout these times, miso played a pivotal role in hearty winter dishes such as Soba Noodles in a Miso Stew. With virtually every local area producing its own miso paste since antiquity, the extent of miso's importance can be judged by the sentimental expression *temai-miso*. More than a homage to the miso of one's own area, it implies the emotions expressed by the English expression "There's no place like home."

There are three basic miso types: sweet, medium salty, and salty. In general, white miso is sweet; dark miso is salty. Color ranges along a spectrum from something near ivory to a dark amber, and the salt content varies from about 3 to 15 percent.

Various kinds of miso are now being exported to or made in the United States. In fact, American miso companies have sprung up at a grass-roots level and supply multiple flavors and varieties. Professionals as well as housewives often make blends, easily done by grinding a combination of different pastes in a mortar for a minute or two and experimenting until the desired color and taste are achieved. Once the miso has been opened, store it in an airtight container and refrigerate. White miso keeps approximately 3 months; red, longer.

**Mountain yam (*yama imo*):** A variety of potato, shaped like a dog's paw. It has a sweet taste and can be grated to a glutinous consistency.

It is the glutinous texture which makes it the ideal binding agent in Groat and

Mountain Yam Fry. Like daikon, it is considered to be an excellent digestive. Mountain yam is now available at many Japanese food outlets in the United States. The standard sweet yam is not a substitute.

*Natto*: This rich soybean product with a cheeselike flavor is still underestimated, unappreciated, and misunderstood, mainly because the sticky "threads" resulting from its special fermentation process are strong and stubborn, making it pretty tricky for beginners to eat. *Natto* can be made easily at home with soybeans, *"natto* spore" (now available at major health-food dealers on both coasts), a pot, and a box. Place the cooked beans in a box, sprinkle with the spore, and let sit overnight. The cooked and "seeded" beans will turn into a fresh batch of the slightly caramel-tasting *natto.* If allowed to sit too long on store shelves, the beans become overripe. Although you cannot check the quality until you open up the package at home, the best *natto* should have a light, tannish color and still be moist and a little puffy. Too dark a color indicates overripening and a correspondingly bitter taste. To remedy this situation somewhat, stir the beans together with chopsticks or a spoon and combine with chopped onions, *wasabi* horseradish, and soy sauce. Since this food is the result of bacterial action, no preservative can be used. Thus, *natto* should be eaten as soon as possible.

**Nori seaweed:** Everyone who has eaten sushi is familiar with these crisp, paper-thin sheets of dried seaweed. Nori is as indispensable to the soba-maker as it is to the sushi-maker. Its importance in making Soba Sushi, for example, is easily understood, but its aromatic fragrance, bright sheen, and dark, blackish purple color, with a hint of green, add a special touch to most soba dishes. It is used in virtually all the cold and many of the hot noodle recipes in this book. Nori is best stored in a tightly sealed can to keep out moisture and sunlight. Precut strips of toasted nori and flavored nori are also on the market, but it is better to use standard-size sheets, toasting and cutting them yourself just before using to capture their distinctive fragrance.

To toast a sheet of nori, pass the sheet of nori seaweed back and forth over a medium flame several times. Within 10 to 15 seconds, the surface will become shiny and the nori will emit a nice fragrance. Turn off the heat and tear the sheet into bite-size pieces.

*Okara*: One of Japan's most neglected foods (even in Japan), *okara* is the ground soybean pulp that remains after the curd has been drained away. It should be used the same day it is made, and so is best obtained from a local tofu-maker or distributor.

*Okara* combines well with foods with strong flavors, as it has very little flavor of its own. Keep wrapped and refrigerated until ready to use.

**Potato starch (*katakuriko*):** This is a starch made from the sweet or white potato. It is used to make thick, clear sauces, but should be used only in dishes that are going to be eaten the same day, as it "leaks" water. Since potato starch is stronger than cornstarch, substitute 1½ Tbsps cornstarch for 1 Tbsp potato starch.

**Salmon roe (*ikura*):** Used in Western as well as Eastern countries for its taste and bright orange color, salmon roe was once discarded in the United States. Now, of course, it has found favor as a sushi topping. Similarly, it makes an ideal topping for Soba Sushi or for a simple bowl of noodles in broth.

**Sesame seeds:** There are various uses for sesame seeds in soba cookery. As a garnish, they lend a nutty fragrance and are thus used to help bring out the sweetness of, say, the *natto* in the Cold Soba Noodles with *Natto* and Sesame recipe. Another use is to grind the seeds into a paste and mix it into the chilled dipping sauce with a touch of freshly grated ginger, creating a refreshing sauce sure to ease the dog days of summer.

There are both white and black sesame. Black sesame has a slightly stronger flavor, while the white is slightly more oily. When using sesame as a garnish, choose the color that looks best—black on green vegetables, either white or black on rice, and so on.

Try to obtain the whole seed, as once it is cracked open, it can easily go rancid. Therefore, keep seeds in an airtight container free from moisture.

**Seven-flavor spice (*shichimi togarashi* ):** This aromatic mixture of spices is composed of red pepper flakes, dried mandarin peel, white poppy seed, powdered *sansho*, hemp seed, and *shiso* or green nori seaweed. It is great on any of the hot noodle dishes and is a standard condiment at any soba shop.

**Shiitake mushroom:** This versatile brown mushroom is available in both fresh and dried forms: The fresh variety is now being cultivated and sold in some markets in the United States, and the dried kind is widely available in Oriental food stores. Black Chinese mushrooms are a good substitute and may, in fact, be the same thing, although reference books are vague. Ordinary white mushrooms are totally different in flavor and aroma, but will do if nothing else is available.

When buying fresh shiitake, look for caps that are curled under, not opened out. The undersides of the caps should be whitish. Brown or mottled undersides indicate old mushrooms. The thicker the mushroom, the better. Some get so thick that the tops of the caps split and crack, and these are the best quality. There are spring and fall crops, but the spring mushrooms are better, with thicker flesh and a stronger aroma.

Dried mushrooms are sold whole, cut into strips, and in crumbled or powdered form. Thick flesh and good aroma (you can usually sniff and tell if the aroma is good even if packaged in clear plastic) are the criteria for good dried shiitake. Reconstitute in tepid water until soft. Reconstitution time will vary greatly with the thickness and size of the mushrooms, but calculate 2 to 3 hours for good mushrooms. A shorter soaking time is possible if the shiitake are to be used in simmered foods.

Unlike white mushrooms, the stems of shiitake are tough and must be removed from both fresh and dried mushrooms. Reserve these for soup stock if you wish.

**Shiso:** Although two varieties exist, the green variety is by far the most often used at soba establishments. It accompanies many of the appetizers served at the high-class soba restaurants and is used in making Flavored Soba Noodles. It is also used for its minty and aromatic fragrance, which seems to fit soba like a glove.

**Soy sauce:** Soy sauce is made from soybeans, wheat, and a salt-water mixture. It is the major ingredient in the broth that accompanies soba noodles in Japan. Like miso and saké, several varieties have been developed over the centuries. In addition to the so-called regular dark-colored soy sauce, lighter, milder (low-sodium for those who must restrict their intake of salt), and even sweet soy sauce have joined the ranks of standard everyday products on store shelves.

Soy sauce, like anything homemade, emits a fragrance all its own. It contains a high percentage of amino acids, notably glutamine acid (also present in *konbu*), which lends this seasoning its distinctive and pleasing taste.

The recipes in this book call for regular or occasionally light-colored soy sauce. These sauces are made in the traditional way, which entails a six-to-twelve-month fermentation period. The process can be speeded up by adding alcohol (for example), thereby shortening the fermentation to a period of three months or less. In addition, these recipes have been conceived with naturally brewed Japanese soy sauce in mind, and Chinese soy sauce will not work. Beware also of synthetic soy sauces, often with Chinese-sounding names, that use additional ingredients to hasten the fermentation process. Needless to say, these are not the varieties that will yield a soba broth worth raving about here.

Actually, I had the chance to prepare homemade soy sauce while living with Mr. Noboru Muramoto (author of *Healing Ourselves*) from 1971 to 1975. As in cultivating a garden, you must attend to it faithfully, stirring it twice a day (morning and night) to ensure the proper blending of the ingredients. After about three months the whole garage started to exude the sweetest caramel-like fragrance. Scooping out some of the "living" soy-wheat mixture and using it in bread-making not only makes it into a meal in itself but also works as a "natural" rising agent in place of yeast. Although you may balk at making your own soy sauce, the results are worth the effort. Grass-roots production of soy sauce is still in its infancy in America, but it's possible to buy a wide variety of quality soy sauce products made by Kikkoman.

**Thin deep-fried tofu,** *see* **tofu, thin deep-fried.**

**Tofu:** The history of soybean cuisine in America began with grass-roots efforts a little more than fifteen years ago. The ever-adaptable soybean stands proud as a giant industry in the United States today. Having sprung up in towns across the nation, tofu-makers continue to break new ground with such adaptations as the New York–born tofutti (ice cream made from soybeans and natural flavorings). With ingenuity like this, other nutritious and scrumptious uses of the soybean will undoubtedly emerge.

The sizes of tofu cakes in the United States apparently vary. Of the various types of tofu used in soba cuisine, deep-fried tofu of different kinds (see below) is used most often. The Soy-Soba Noodle recipe calls for soaked and mashed raw soybeans, but in the northern country area of Iwate, a block of regular or "cotton" tofu is added directly into the buckwheat flour with 2 or 3 egg yolks and, with only a little water, is mixed together into a dough. Store tofu blocks in clean water and use within 2 days, changing the water often.

**Tofu, thin deep-fried (*abura-age, usu-age*):** This ingredient appears frequently in soba cooking, but the most famous use is in the dish "Fox" (*Kitsune*) Soba. In Japan, as in the West, foxes are thought to be keen and cunning and somewhat daring. The connection is that these characteristics were also necessary for temple cooks, who constantly had to create ways of preparing food that would satisfy like meat without containing any. Since this fried variety of tofu is rich in oil, when cooked together with the flavoring sauce it takes on a rich and sweet, baconlike taste, satisfying the eater without any sense of lack. (See Fox

Soba for preparation.) Thin deep-fried tofu should be sealed in plastic wrap and refrigerated. It will keep 1 week in this manner. Larger amounts will keep 2 to 3 months if frozen.

*Wakame* seaweed: This green, ribbonlike sea vegetable's slippery-smooth texture and delightful fragrance make it extremely popular, and in fact *Wakame Soba* is served at a great majority of the stand-up soba shops throughout Japan. Soak as you would *konbu* and allow to cook in the broth for 2 to 3 minutes. It also combines well with salads or appetizers, and in this book is called for in the Groat Salad with Vinegar Dressing.

A superb health food rich in calcium, fresh *wakame* appears on the market only in the spring, but dried *wakame* is available year-round. There are a number of varieties, but in every case the best *wakame* should have a dark, blackish green color. Store in cellophane in a cool, dark place.

*Wasabi* horseradish: By no means the exclusive domain of the sushi-maker, this variety of horseradish is indispensable to soba cuisine as well. Releasing a sharp, tangy taste when grated into paste, *wasabi* is a standard condiment to accompany cool dishes. Together with white radish and long onions, it forms the trio of garnishes that are considered so essential to soba cuisine that they are simply referred to as "the three tastes" (*san-shoku*) by shops in Tokyo.

There are two kinds of *wasabi*: that produced in the clear-mountain-water areas and that which grows in the fields. The former is the variety that is by and large in supply and demand.

The *wasabi* root is green in color, strong in fragrance, and, when grated, hot and spicy. Compared with field *wasabi*, that produced in clear mountain water has obviously superior characteristics. While the former has a dry, harsh taste, the latter acquires a fine balance between its pungent and sweet qualities.

To grate the *wasabi* root, first cut off the top leaves and sharpen the head like shaving a pencil. Scrape the hard, impacted dirt and skin off the portion to be grated using the dull side of a knife. Using a sturdy metal grater, grind from top to bottom.

Once the *wasabi* is grated, it keeps for only a short time. Since about 15 to 20 portions can be obtained from one root, you probably won't use a whole one at a time, except for a party. Therefore, after grating the portion needed, it is necessary for the remaining part to be stored. By placing it in a bin of cool water, you can keep it from losing its fragrance for at least 24 hours.

Because the fresh root is so expensive, powdered *wasabi* has become an acceptable alternative. Powdered *wasabi* is made from a different type of horseradish and includes cayenne pepper (*togarashi* in Japan). Consequently, it is sharper and less subtle than fresh *wasabi*. To use, add enough water to make a thick paste, then cover for ten minutes to allow the flavor to mature.

*Yuzu* citron: This unique variety of citron originated in China. Belonging to the orange family, its tall evergreen tree produces a yellow fruit in winter and one that is green in early autumn. Only its outer skin is used, as the fruit itself is too bitter. The zest, on the other hand, imparts a fruity "sweet-lemon" type of taste and fragrance.

Put into chilled broth, it enhances the light and refreshing feeling of the broth. When put into hot broth, it creates a delicately aromatic fragrance. In addition, it is said to be effective in lightening the oily feeling of dishes containing fish or animal products, and therefore is almost always used in soba dishes with tempura, chicken, or duck.

Generally the zest is peeled off in a round, semicircular motion, piece by piece. The size of the piece, left up to each master's sense, is either as big as a nickel or as small as a sunflower seed. When used to accompany side dishes, it is often peeled extra large, thinly sliced, and piled on top of the crisp tempura or lightly fried and seasoned chicken. A very simple, refreshing side dish, traditionally served in Japanese cooking, is made simply by combining finely sliced *yuzu* zest together with grated daikon radish. When *nameko* mushrooms (small, tasty mushrooms floating in their own syrup) are added, this becomes *nameko-oroshi*, also a standard side dish of great popularity. In like manner, *yuzu* can be added as that "something extra" to give Western salads a little more zest.

One of its most unusual uses, however, is to put its completely peeled and separated skin in a food processor and then knead it together with the highly refined, pure-white *sarashina* buckwheat flour. This combination produces a popular variety among the style of buckwheat noodles known as *kawari soba* (see Flavored Soba Noodles). It provides a noodle with a refreshing hint of citrus taste and a beautiful bright-yellow color. (Only the yellow winter variety is used for this style of noodles.) Once again, taking a hint from this method try adding blended *yuzu* into breads, cookies, cakes, or pastries.

# II

# ABOUT
# SOBA

*In the first year, I thought the taste of soba came from the skill of the cook.*

*In the second, I thought it came from the ingenuity and technique of the miller.*

*In the seventh year I finally understood that the sweetness of soba is largely decided in the fields.*

# Nutrition

$S$oba noodles provide the best of two worlds. First, they provide a quick source of high-quality nutrition and boast a superior protein makeup, and contain an abundance of vitamin $B_1$, vitamin P (with the valuable flavanoid rutin known for its effectiveness in reducing the cholesterol count in the blood), and dietary fiber. Secondly, while the word *pasta* connotes calorie and weight gain in the minds of many people, soba noodles are virtually fat-free. By consuming one large portion of noodles per day (7 ounces) and a piece of fresh fruit or a salad, an abundance of utilizable high-quality protein and close to 40 percent of the recommended adult daily requirement of vitamin B can be obtained. In the text that follows buckwheat's merits will be explored by examining not only the latest scientific research but also a centuries-old Buddhist training tradition in which buckwheat plays a part. In addition, the discussion will cover dietary fiber, vitamin P and rutin, colin (which helps facilitate the functioning of the liver), and vitamins $B_1$ and $B_2$, and lipids and minerals. It is no wonder that for centuries soba has been a popular traditional item of Japanese cuisine.

Buckwheat's nutritional and medicinal value was intuited long before the twentieth century. An entry in one of the earliest known nutritional/folk-medicinal references concerning buckwheat in Japan, the *Honcho shoku kan* (*Food Dictionary*), published in 1697, reads: "Buckwheat is sweet, contains no poison, relaxes the nerves, eases irritability, and helps to clear out and release old feces from the stomach and intestines."

In a modern work of the same nature, *Kampo shokumotsu seishitsu to koyo* (*Herbs and Food Character and Effectiveness*), the text is even more specific: "Soba is a very nourishing food which works to relax the body, helps relieve and prevent inflammation, excessive perspiration, nosebleed, or high blood pressure; and helps maintain a good functioning of the intestine by helping to remove old feces from the intestines."

Interestingly enough, one of today's top soba historians and authors, Shigeru Niijima, notes that the popular Japanese custom of eating buckwheat on the last day of the year (*toshikoshi soba*), which continues to this day, served a dual purpose. Not only did the quick, fortifying meal give merchants and others with busy year-end schedules a burst of needed energy to complete their last-minute chores, they benefited from buckwheat's cleansing of the digestive tract. That is, buckwheat helped them to start the New Year off with a clean slate physically as well as mentally.

The custom of eating buckwheat on the last day of the year can be traced all the way back to the Kamakura period (1185–1333), long before the advent of soba noodles "just" four hundred years ago. Originally, buckwheat was made into dumplings and used as a portable food for ninja and ascetics who spent extended periods of time training or traveling in remote mountain areas. Having very few or no sophisticated cooking utensils available, they would cook dumplings and carry them for the next few days' meals. In emergencies or when no cooking utensils were available at all, they would dissolve buckwheat flour in water and drink it. As buckwheat requires little cooking, keeps well, can even be reheated, and most importantly was found to contain enough nutrition to sustain a traveler through his rigors, it was ideal for those times of austerity when stamina was a must.

One of the most intriguing accounts of Japan's traditional reliance on buckwheat was given at The Second International Buckwheat Symposium held in Kyushu, Japan, in 1983. Presented by the Reverend Shocho Hagami of the Mt. Hiei Buddhist sanctuary; the account links buckwheat with the demanding practice of *kaiho-gyo*, a Buddhist rite.

## MT. HIEI AND BUCKWHEAT

About twelve hundred years ago when Kyoto was the political and cultural center of Japan, the master priest Dengyo Saicho set up a sanctuary on Mt. Hiei and erected the Enryaku-ji temple, establishing the home of the Tendai sect of Buddhism. Saicho was born in a hamlet of Sakamoto on the eastern side of Mt. Hiei, which overlooks both Kyoto and the neighboring prefecture of Shiga. In A.D. 766, at the age of 19, he hiked deep into the mountains, built a thatched hut, and began a life of meditation and discipline. At 38 he undertook a voyage to China. China at that time was a formidable power and a great cultural center in the East. Saicho studied there for only six months but returned to Japan with a rich knowledge of esoteric teachings, Zen doctrines, and many other precepts, including the orthodox Tendai philosophy.

Soon after his return, he set up the Tendai sect at Mt. Hiei, which become one of the pillars of Japanese Buddhism. Almost concurrently he become the first priest to be given the title of master by the imperial court.

The Mt. Hiei sanctuary is well known for its austere disciplines. The most austere are walking training (*kaiho-gyo*), burning-of-wooden-sticks training (*goma-gyo*), and seclusion training (*rozan-gyo*). (*Gyo* means training.) The latter was established by Saicho and has been transmitted down to the present over eleven centuries. For a period of twelve years of seclusion in the mountains, a priest in rozan-gyo devotes himself to the service of Buddha, dressing in simple robes and living on a frugal diet; he observes almost unbearably strict commandments and daily exercises in an inclement environment, often at the risk of his life.

Kaiho-gyo is a discipline to be observed in prayer for the attainment of higher spiritual powers as described in a chapter of the Lotus Sutra. It entails a strict discipline requiring the priest to walk the peaks and glens to visit many places of worship over the course of 1,000 days. These days of self-discipline are divided into ten segments of 100 days each, and it takes seven years to complete the ten rounds. (The first three years may be called the preparation period, when only one round of 100 days of 18-plus miles a day is allowed.) Making two rounds a year is compulsory in the fourth and fifth year, which adds up to 700 days in five years. Up until the seven-hundredth day a priest is supposed to walk up and down 18 miles every day, chant sutras, and perform other rituals at the pre-designated 300-odd spots, including temples and historic ruins. Immediately after the seven-hundredth day the priest confines himself in the Meio-do hall for nine days, where he chants a set prayer 100,000 times without eating any food, without drinking a drop of water, and without lying down to rest or sleeping a wink. This is the preliminary goma-gyo. In the eighth round of walking, the distance to be covered in one day is doubled, with an additional discipline of walking up the steep Kihara slope to the Ishiyama temple (a temple at the western foot of Mt. Hiei) and back. In the ninth round the distance is extended to 52 miles. During the 100 days of the final round the walking is reduced to the original distance of 18 miles.

After the successful completion of this 1,000-day discipline, buckwheat comes to the fore. To purify himself for the final training—one last round of goma-gyo—the priest must first undertake a 100-day fast called *gokoku-dachi*. *Gokoku* refers to five basic staples: rice, barley, wheat, soybean, and adzuki beans; *-dachi* means abstinence. The priest is not to ingest any grains or beans, nor is he allowed to take salt. Since eating any kind of animal food is prohibited in Buddhism, he eats no staple food that is considered necessary for subsistence from the viewpoint of modern nutritional science. *But there is one exception to the rules: he is allowed to eat buckwheat.*

Certainly hundreds of years of folk knowledge and remedies played a part in selecting buckwheat for its role in gokoku-dachi. Another factor may have been buckwheat's ability to grow and even flourish at higher altitudes. Mt. Hiei's elevation (2,750 feet) makes it an almost ideal place for cultivating the grain. In any case buckwheat had already proven itself many times before the Reverend Hagami began kaiho-gyo at the age of 45 in 1947 and completed goma-gyo at 51 in 1953. Even at the ripe age of 81 he remains confident that the centuries-old training speaks for itself, as he concludes "I dare to say that the process is absolutely rational and scientific."

Although successful completion of this training depends mainly on the daily effort and courage of the disciple, modern research on the subject of buckwheat supplies an abundance of convincing evidence to affirm its nutritional value. I want to add here that in compiling the following report I am indebted for much of the information to Dr. Keisuke Tsuji of the National Institute of Nutrition (Japan); Ivan Kreft and Branka Javornik of the University of Ljubljana (Yugoslavia); and Bjorn Eggum of the National Institute of Animal Science (Denmark).

PROTEIN AND AMINO ACIDS

Among buckwheat's many fine qualities, perhaps its excellent amino-acid composition stands out above the rest. Of the twenty or more amino acids needed for the human body to function properly, eight to ten are termed "essential amino acids," as they cannot be synthesized or produced by our bodies and so must be obtained from our daily food. A food's value as a protein source depends not just on the total amount of protein it has, but also on the amount of protein the body can use. This amount is referred to as the Net Protein Utilization, or NPU.

From the specialist's point of view, eggs are considered to be an almost perfect protein food. That is, eggs contain all of the essential amino acids in the highest and most well-balanced proportions and have an NPU of 94. By comparison, buckwheat is ranked at 74, wheat germ 67, beef 67, chicken 65, soybeans 61, and wheat 47 (Fig. 1).

| Food | NPU (percentage) | Food | NPU (percentage) |
|---|---|---|---|
| Eggs | 94% | Hamburger | 67% |
| Pork | 82 | Oatmeal | 66 |
| Fish | 80 | Tofu | 65 |
| Cottage cheese | 75 | Chicken | 65 |
| Buckwheat flour | 74 | Soybeans, soy flour | 61 |
| Brown rice | 70 | Wheat flour | 47 |
| Cheese | 70 | Peanuts | 43 |
| Wheat germ | 67 | Lentils | 30 |
| Beef (steak) | 67 | | |

Fig. 1.　Net Protein Utilization Scores

Although animal foods (including dairy products) occupy the upper rankings, they also carry with them high levels of fat and cholesterol. Buckwheat's score of 74 indicates that the body can utilize all but 26 percent of the available protein. This score does not reflect the fact that 17 percent of the nonprotein substance is high-crude fiber, which is only now receiving attention for its essential role in the human diet (see Dietary Fiber).

A breakdown of the protein by amino acids (Fig. 2) reveals that buckwheat contains high amounts of lysine. Lysine is important for its ability to help the body utilize and convert protein. It is often present in only small amounts in plant protein. Eggum acknowledges the role that foods high in lysine play when combined with grain, for example:

> It is a general assumption that the quality of animal protein is better than protein of plant origin. This is a very general statement as several vegetable proteins, e.g., protein from buckwheat, can be of very high quality. However, it is true that animal proteins in most cases have a high lysine content. Furthermore, the digestibility of animal products is in general very high.
>
> . . . animal proteins have a high lysine content and will as such have a positive complementary effect on protein quality in diets based on cereals.

Buckwheat's protein works in the same way. When wheat is combined with buckwheat, as in the noodle-making process (wheat acts as a binding agent), the soba noodle attains an NPU of 81 due to the high lysine content. By combining soba, wheat, and soybeans (see Soy-Soba Noodles), an NPU rivaling that of eggs is possible.

Fig. 2.   Protein Quality in Grains and Animals Foods

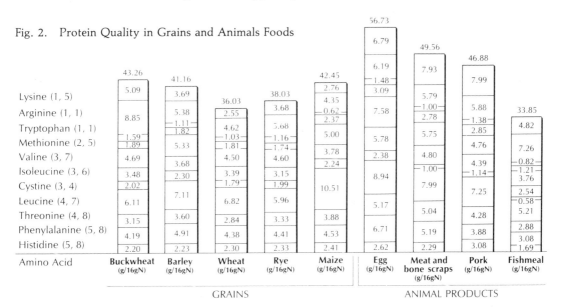

| Amino Acid | Buckwheat (g/16gN) | Barley (g/16gN) | Wheat (g/16gN) | Rye (g/16gN) | Maize (g/16gN) | Egg (g/16gN) | Meat and bone scraps (g/16gN) | Pork (g/16gN) | Fishmeal (g/16gN) |
|---|---|---|---|---|---|---|---|---|---|
| (Total) | 43.26 | 41.16 | 36.03 | 38.03 | 42.45 | 56.73 | 49.56 | 46.88 | 33.85 |
| Lysine (1, 5) | 5.09 | 3.69 | 2.55 | 3.68 | 2.76 | 6.79 | 7.93 | 7.99 | 4.82 |
| Arginine (1, 1) | 8.85 | 5.38 | 4.62 | 5.68 | 4.35 | 6.19 | 5.79 | 5.88 | 7.26 |
| Tryptophan (1, 1) | 1.59 | 1.11 | 1.03 | 1.16 | 0.62 | 1.48 | 1.00 | 1.38 | 0.82 |
| Methionine (2, 5) | 1.89 | 1.82 | 1.81 | 1.74 | 2.37 | 3.09 | 2.78 | 2.85 | 1.21 |
| Valine (3, 7) | 4.69 | 5.33 | 4.50 | 4.60 | 5.00 | 7.58 | 5.75 | 4.76 | 3.76 |
| Isoleucine (3, 6) | 3.48 | 3.68 | 3.39 | 3.15 | 3.78 | 5.78 | 4.80 | 4.39 | 2.54 |
| Cystine (3, 4) | 2.02 | 2.30 | 1.79 | 1.99 | 2.24 | 2.38 | 1.00 | 1.14 | 0.58 |
| Leucine (4, 7) | 6.11 | 7.11 | 6.82 | 5.96 | 10.51 | 8.94 | 7.99 | 7.25 | 5.21 |
| Threonine (4, 8) | 3.15 | 3.60 | 2.84 | 3.33 | 3.88 | 5.17 | 5.04 | 4.28 | 2.88 |
| Phenylalanine (5, 8) | 4.19 | 4.91 | 4.38 | 4.41 | 4.53 | 6.71 | 5.19 | 3.88 | 3.08 |
| Histidine (5, 8) | 2.20 | 2.23 | 2.30 | 2.33 | 2.41 | 2.62 | 2.29 | 3.08 | 1.69 |

GRAINS                                    ANIMAL PRODUCTS

**Source:** Eggum, "The Protein Quality of Buckwheat in Comparison with Other Protein Sources of Plant or Animal Origin." (1980)

NOTE: The first set of figures in parentheses ranks buckwheat's amino acid against those of the listed grains. The second set of figures indicates buckwheat's ranking inclusive of the protein-rich animal products.

Allowing for small fluctuations due to the variety of the plant and the growing conditions, "the concentration of lysine in buckwheat is almost always above 5 percent, reaching the ideal level of lysine in proteins proposed by FAO/WHO group" (Kreft). This is roughly twice the amount of lysine in either wheat or white rice.

Compared with brown and well-milled white rice, buckwheat noodles (with 35 percent wheat) contain 9.7 percent protein by weight (brown rice contains 7.4 percent and white rice 6.8 percent), or roughly 1.5 times the protein found in white rice. When cooked, the figures are 4.8 percent, 3.3 percent, and 2.6 percent respectively. This difference is considerable. Buckwheat groats and dumplings score even higher.

## VITAMIN P AND RUTIN

When we think about the important vitamins present in buckwheat, vitamin P, containing the valuable flavonoid rutin, stands out as one of buckwheat's most important characteristics. In Japan and China, it has been known for generations that buckwheat is an effective preventative measure against high blood pressure. This is due to the rutin present in buckwheat but absent in grains.

Rutin is known to keep the capillaries and arteries strong and flexible, protecting the body against the internal and external bleeding and hemorrhages which may accompany old age. It also protects the blood vessels from rupturing or forming clots.

Today, medicine containing rutin together with vitamin C is used to treat high blood pressure, arteriosclerosis, and purpura (a seepage of blood into the skin and mucous membranes, resulting in purplish discoloration). Thus, by combining buckwheat with foods high in vitamin C (which buckwheat lacks), the effectiveness of the rutin in buckwheat is strengthened.

Buckwheat flour in its raw state contains about 6.5 mg of rutin per 100 g. Although the amount of rutin remains constant regardless of growing conditions, it decreases slightly when exposed to heat and light. Boiled buckwheat contains 1.2 mg of rutin per 100 g. Rutin, like vitamins $B_1$ and $B_2$, dissolves easily in water. Fortunately, in the case of soba noodles, the cooking water, or *soba-yu*, is served to the customer near the end of the meal. To receive the full benefit of the nutrition contained in buckwheat noodles, it is essential to drink this cooking water as a final part of the eating process. Combined with a little of the leftover broth, this provides a most satisfying sweet soup while aiding in the digestion of the meal.

## VITAMINS $B_1$ AND $B_2$

In addition to vitamin P, buckwheat contains considerable amounts of vitamins $B_1$ and $B_2$. The former plays an important role in rekindling energy by facilitating the working of the nerves. It is also effective in cases of exhaustion, irritability, and loss of appetite. Vitamin $B_2$ assists the lipids in their work (see below). If taken together with vitamin E, it becomes an effective precaution against hardening of the arteries (arteriosclerosis).

Cooked soba noodles have about two times more vitamin $B_1$ than cooked white rice. If we mix hot water into buckwheat flour and beat it into the form of dumplings, thereby eating buckwheat without losing any of its valuable water-soluble elements (including vitamin $B_1$) during the boiling process, we can provide 40 percent of the daily adult requirement of vitamin $B_1$ by eating only 100 grams (or about one-quarter of a pound) of buckwheat.

In *Soba Technique* by Kazuo Fujimura, the author mentions in his nutrition chapter that during the Edo Period, beriberi was prevalent. At the time, the people of Tokyo were terrified of the disease. Though they knew not its cause, they somehow knew enough to eat soba noodles, which they did often and with a passion. Fittingly, they earned the label "soba crazy" from outsiders.

Vitamin $B_2$ occurs in buckwheat flour in an amount only about one-fourth that of $B_1$ (0.11 mg $B_2$ per 100 g buckwheat flour, as opposed to 0.46 mg $B_1$). Yet, that is almost twice the amount in brown rice (0.6 mg) and four times that of white rice (0.3 mg).

DIETARY FIBER

Dietary fiber is a carbohydrate that is not easily assimilated or digested; yet, it is now being recognized as playing an essential role in the prevention of many adult diseases now afflicting many Western countries. Dr. Dennis Burkitt, a surgeon and epidemiologist on the British Medical Research Council, is credited with starting this new trend of thought. Two decades of study and work in a hospital in Africa, where the diet is high in fiber, led him to the conclusion that an intestinal disorder known as diverticulosis is caused by a diet consisting of too many refined carbohydrates. In 1972 he supported his earlier findings with another study that stated that a decrease in dietary fiber in the diet corresponds to high incidences of cardiovascular disease, appendicitis, gallbladder disease, hernia, and colon cancer.

At Chiba University in Japan, several experiments have been carried out on rats to see what effect, if any, the addition of buckwheat, with its high percentage of fiber, into the diet may have on the level of cholesterol in the blood. In one experiment, a group of rats (Group A) was fed a diet of 55 percent raw buckwheat, the above-mentioned 0.5 percent cholesterol, and other nutrients that were kept constant for both groups. The rats in Group B were given a diet consisting of 55 percent raw wheat. (All other factors remained the same.) In an analogous test, cooked soba noodles (made from 45 percent buckwheat and 55 percent wheat) were substituted for the raw buckwheat in Group A, and cooked *hiya-mugi* (a noodle made only from wheat) was substituted for the raw wheat in Group B. In both experiments, it was reported that Group A— the group fed buckwheat—recorded considerably lower levels of cholesterol in the blood. Furthermore, the proportion of cholesterol with a high concentration of lipoproteins increased. From the specialist's point of view, cholesterol is known to have either low (often very low) or high amounts of lipoproteins. While the types of cholesterol with low lipoprotein levels are carried over into the cells of the blood vessels (known to be a main factor in cases of cerebral hemorrhaging and heart attacks), the type of cholesterol with a high density of lipoproteins is removed from the cell membranes.

Fiber reduces serum cholesterol and neutral fat because fiber increases bile discharge to the intestine at the same time that cholesterol is discharged. Cardiovascular disease and cerebrovascular diseases are caused by cholesterol and/or neutral fat deposits inside the blood vessels. Therefore the incidence of heart disease in rural Africa is relatively low, since people there have less cholesterol and fat in their blood.

Such research is still being conducted, and buckwheat continues to make a strong showing. Further studies that will help us to improve our diet and provide us with protective measures against such adult diseases as high blood pressure, diabetes, and cerebral hemorrhaging are eagerly awaited.

### LIPIDS

By now it has become evident that buckwheat, among other things, helps the body eliminate unwanted cholesterol. As a footnote to the above discussion, a look at the lipids in buckwheat is appropriate.

Buckwheat contains 2 to 3 percent lipids, which are distributed mainly within the embryo and secondarily within the endosperm. Close to 30 percent of these lipids (also known as fatty acids) are made up of the valuable and main essential fatty acid, linoleic acid. Nutritionally speaking, linoleic acid is known to help decrease blood cholesterol levels and provide protection against the coagulation of blood within the blood vessels. In addition, it has a low level of free fatty acid, which means that it does not change or putrify even if stored for a long period.

The lipids in buckwheat also contain abundant amounts of physiologically effective plant sterol (0.2 percent). This percentage is largely made up of sitosterol, stigmasterol, and campesterol. The main physiological effects of these sterols is to prevent cholesterol from increasing in the blood serum, as well as to absorb cholesterol within the small intestine.

### MINERALS

Potassium, magnesium, phosphate, and iron are abundant in buckwheat flour (especially in grades 2 and 3 of Japanese flour). Generally speaking, soybeans and other beans are noted for their potassium and magnesium content, another demonstration of buckwheat's resemblance to the bean family. Of special interest is that buckwheat contains more iron than grains. These minerals play an essential role in the prevention of hypertension and anemia.

Another effective element within buckwheat is colin, which facilitates the working of the liver. Although excessive drinking places a burden on the liver, drinking on occasion and within reason is one of the pleasures of life. Depending on how much and how often one drinks, of course, colin will to some extent assist in preventing excess fat from collecting in the liver (that is, assist in the prevention of fatty-acid buildup, a problem for people who consume too much alcohol). In addition, the methionine and niacin in buckwheat also work to help the liver; therefore it is said not only in jest that soba is an ally of the habitual drinker.

## BUCKWHEAT AND OTHER FOODS

By combining small amounts of egg, tempura, chicken, or vegetable with a bowl of soba noodles and then garnishing it with the mineral-rich condiments that accompany soba cuisine, a nutritional meal that approaches the ideal balance of nutrients can be made. In addition to the traditional hot and cold soba noodles, the variety of other dishes—the soba dumpling, buckwheat cookies and crackers, and soba sushi—provide us with a wealth of menu ideas to enjoy.

In both the United States and Japan the Chinese-style ramen noodle is becoming increasingly popular, even though it has no where near soba's nutrients and versatility.

By adding the ever-adaptable buckwheat to Western or even Chinese cooking, this traditional food could capture the fancy and recognition of young and old alike. Dr. Tsuji put it best when he said that he hoped "buckwheat would graduate from its position in the hands of the soba professional to reach its deserved status as a food valued and used by all for its nutrition and inherent sweet taste."

# Buckwheat: From Seed to Table

Common buckwheat (*Fagopyrum esculentum*), the main character in this book, is one of about fifteen species within the genus *Fagopyrum*. The name comes from the Latin *fagus*, "beech," and the Greek *pyros*, "wheat," and alludes to the seeds being shaped like those of beech trees, or beech-mast, whence came their name from the German *buchweizen*, "beechwheat." This genus belongs to the family of Polygonaceae "which includes various species of sorrel and dock (*rumex*), and of smartweed, knotweed, bindweed (*polygonum*), all more or less troublesome weeds" (Hunt). Quite clearly, buckwheat is a different breed of plant than the normal cereal grains of rice, wheat, millet, rye, and oats, which all belong to the family of Gramineae.

There are two principal varieties of common buckwheat grown in the United States and Canada, silverhull and Japanese, from which a great majority of the buckwheat groats and flour products come (Coe). These varieties or similar ones are cultivated mainly in the northern hemispheric countries of China, Russia, Canada, the United States, Nepal, India, Japan, and Korea, and are also a crop of some importance in Yugoslavia, Poland, Hungary, Brazil, South Africa, and other countries of the African continent. More recently, it has been cultivated in Austria, Switzerland, Italy, France, and Great Britain.

Able to grow within the unusually short span of 75 days, buckwheat is easily cultivated twice a year: "summer" buckwheat (planted in late May or early June, harvested in August) and "autumn" buckwheat (planted in late July or early August, harvested in October). In general the latter variety is known to have superior taste and fragrance due to the cooler temperatures at night. By and large, autumn buckwheat is the variety which makes its way to the shelves of our supermarkets and health-food stores.

The second variety, *F. tataricum*, referred to variously as "Tartary buckwheat," "Indian wheat," or "rye buckwheat," "is grown to a limited extent in the mountains of North Carolina, in Maine, in New York, and in a number of other places in the United States and Canada, as well as being reported as growing in the Himalayas of northeastern India and China under cooler and harsher climatic conditions, to which it is better adapted than common buckwheat" (Coe). As its nickname "bitter

Common buckwheat                Tartary buckwheat                Wild or perennial buckwheat

buckwheat" implies, its taste and milling qualities do not compare favorably with the common varieties. In addition to possessing this slightly unbecoming characteristic, it can be clearly distinguished from common buckwheat in a number of ways. The seed is not as angular as that of common buckwheat, and at a quick glance it more closely resembles the seed of a darkish variety of wheat than that of common edible buckwheat. Furthermore, unlike common buckwheat, the flower is lighter and, most importantly, possesses the ability to self-pollinate.

The third main variety is the wild, or perennial, species *F. cymosum*, "the probable ultimate source of both common and Tartary buckwheat, and is native to northern India and China" (Campbell). Its flower, seed shape, and style of pollination resemble common buckwheat. Yet its most commanding characteristic is that it possesses the unwelcome trait of dominating and literally taking over its surroundings. Its yellow-red root increases in size and sends out new sprouts year after year, even if the above-ground portion dies or withers during the winter. Fortunately, it is a special variety that grows only above an elevation of 10,000 feet. Its leaves and roots are used as raw food and herbal teas as they contain a high degree of rutin (see Nutrition).

Since ancient times, both "original" and new strains of buckwheat have been cultivated around the world. (From here on, whenever the word "buckwheat" appears in the text, it will refer to common edible buckwheat.) Having a small whitish or pale pink flower that is an important source of nectar as well as glucoside rutin (Shevchuk, 1983), the branching and weedlike buckwheat plant, which usually grows to a height of 16 to 28 inches, produces a sharp, three-sided seed which turns dark brown when mature. Under the hull of the whole buckwheat grain lies a delicate light-green kernel. These kernels are commonly referred to as buckwheat groats.

Nature has wrapped buckwheat within a hard and tightly clinging hull for good reason. Once removed, buckwheat's treasured fragrance and flavor dissipate within a matter of days. In addition, the color of its hulled seed will change from a pale greenish-yellow to a rich "roasted" brown within three to four weeks. The "roasted-looking" buckwheat which you commonly find in shops is, in many cases, not roasted at all: it has turned color through long exposure to the air. Ideally, buckwheat should be turned into flour on the same day or, at the latest, within three days after hulling.

In Western countries, "buckwheat hulls have very little feed value and are even detrimental as feed for pigs. Most mills burn their hulls. Some, however, sell their hulls as packing material for bottled goods and glass bulbs" (Coe). Interestingly, in Japan, the hull is used as a stuffing for pillows, something akin to the use of feathers in pillows in the West. The cool and light feeling provided by the hull has been a traditional favorite, virtually "imbedding" buckwheat in the Japanese life style.

The plant itself is impressive. Its heart-shaped leaves, maroon-red stalk, white clusters of flowers, and triangular dark brown seeds have inspired more than one Oriental poet. As far back as 812 the verses of the Chinese poet Po Chu-i are recorded:

> Coming out of the gate
> And commanding the wild fields alone,
> Under the light of the shining moon,
> Buckwheat's white flowers
> Look like freshly fallen snow.

One thousand years later the following quotation was credited to Miss Mitford "Village Ser. 1 (1863)": "The beautiful buckwheat, whose transparent leaves and stalks are so brightly tinged with vermilion" (Oxford English Dictionary).

While a field of buckwheat does command one's attention, upon close inspection it is the clusters of dainty five-petaled flowers that are most striking. Yet as attractive as these flowers are, the buckwheat plant itself has many limitations which hinder its potential for self-propagation:

> If the numbers of flowers produced by a buckwheat plant is an indication of the potential seed yield of the plant, then the crop has a large unrealized yield. Studies by several investigators on possible causes of the low seed yield in relation to the number of flowers produced have focused on pollinating agents and on the physiology of reproduction. . . . Free cited several studies, mostly from the U.S.S.R., which gave evidence that buckwheat yields can be increased considerably by the use of honey bees. Marshall found that under controlled conditions buckwheat pollen can be transported by wind. In the U.S.S.R., in the absence of bees it is apparently customary for two persons to drag a rope with sacks attached across

the buckwheat fields, a practice which may be repeated every week or 10 days.

... buckwheat's low seed set is often not the result of a lack of pollen, ... but rather that starch tends to accumulate in the stems of buckwheat, with a very slow rate of digestion and translocation. The translocation of starch to the developing ovaries may therefore be the limiting factor in seed-set. The spraying of growth substances on flowering plants is also reported to have resulted in a higher seed yield. (De Jong)

Since the resulting seed contains the delicate nutritional substance that will be turned into flour, and later into noodles, it is no exaggeration to say that, in searching for the best-quality buckwheat noodles and buckwheat flour, one must study what conditions will produce a superior buckwheat grain.

Moreover, if buckwheat is to yield its unique sweet fragrance and taste, it must be given specific consideration every step of the way— from the harvesting, drying, storing, and shipping stages that it goes through to reach the miller to the continued storing, milling, and shipping stages it undergoes en route to the marketplace, to the final cooking just before it is served at the dinner table.

Aside from its nutritional value, one of buckwheat's attractions as a serviceable food source lies in its ability to grow even in poor soil and in soil where neither rice nor wheat can be cultivated. Although it possesses this ability, the quality of buckwheat is nevertheless influenced by the region and soil.

What, then, are the optimum conditions necessary to produce healthy and tasty buckwheat? Why is it that the flour produced in Japan is sweeter and of a completely different nature than that produced in, say, America and Canada? Are the varieties of buckwheat structurally different, or does the final product differ only because the methods used in taking buckwheat through all its many stages—from the fields to the millers, the millers to the soba makers or market, and from the market to the dinner table—are different? Can this difference of quality be evaluated scientifically?

A valuable hint toward answering the first question can be found by observing the areas in Japan which have long been famous for producing the highest grade of buckwheat. Just as the midwestern states of Iowa, Illinois, and Kansas are renowned as the Corn Belt of America, the areas of Nagano, Kyushu, Hokkaido, Ibaragi, and others are similarly praised as soba areas of Japan. It was noticed long ago that the plots located in the highland or mountain areas produced the best buckwheat. Furthermore, each is situated in an area known to register a substantial difference in temperature between day and night.

Today, it is understood that it is especially important to have cool (but not frosty) temperatures during the period when the flowers are being formed. Otherwise, good-quality buckwheat cannot be expected. For this reason, the area of Togakushi in Nagano has long been recognized as having close to perfect weather conditions for growing buckwheat. The area is often foggy, and even in the summer the temperature rarely exceeds 68°F. Although Kyushu and Hokkaido have become the leading producers of buckwheat in Japan today, the reputation of the Togakushi area for producing top-grade buckwheat still lingers in the minds of the people.

This kind of intuitive wisdom has since been supported by modern scientific research. In "Buckwheat Breeding Perspectives," Yugoslavian agronomist Ivan Kreft states that "for efficient germination and growth of buckwheat, temperatures over 50°F are needed and those of about 68°F seem to be most effective (Sugawara, 1962; Populidi, 1976). Buckwheat is sensitive to temperatures below 34°F. Besides frosts, it is also sensitive to weather that is too warm and dry, especially during the time of flowering. When air temperatures rise above 77°F or 86°F, the flowers begin to wither. . . . Buckwheat can be grown in a variety of soils, including soils poor in nutrients and in stony fields. It is a good utilizer of insoluble phosphorus (Anderson and Thomsen, 1978). When grown in soil too rich in nitrogen, it can easily become lodged."

This leads us to the second question. What are the structural elements within buckwheat that determine its quality? Can these factors be measured scientifically? From the viewpoint of protein content and quality, percentage of fiber, water content, and so on, no clear quantitative differences in their respective makeups could be observed.

Among the experts in Japan, however, there is the opinion that the makeup within the starch structure itself appears to vary according to the region in which buckwheat is grown. That is, the main components of amilose and amilopectine are said to be present in different ratios, according to growing area. It is this difference that is considered to be essential in creating a "real buckwheatlike" taste and texture.

Just how greatly the varieties of edible buckwheat differ from country to country is still under investigation. Yet, in addition to the inevitable differences in the soils of each country, the processing methods must also be taken into account as contributing to or diminishing the taste and fragrance of buckwheat.

Buckwheat undergoes a long journey to get from the field to your table. Let's follow it as it goes from seeding to harvest, observing a few of the many Japanese proverbs about buckwheat along the way.

Buckwheat is sown soon after the danger of spring frosts has passed (in May or June) and harvested before the autumn rains and frost (in August or September). One saying goes: "Within 75 days, soba returns to the soil," meaning that soba can be harvested within that period. Another states curtly: "Soba and half-sandals are made quickly." Half-sandals refers to a traditional sandal used by messengers of old who,

Buckwheat—From Seed to Table

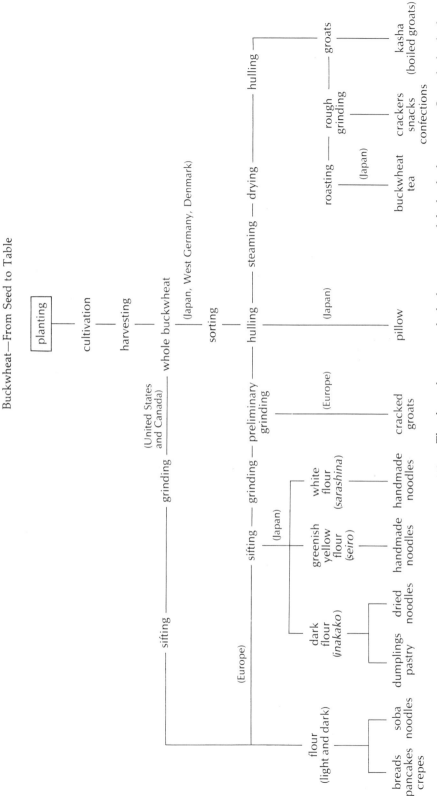

NOTE: The chart above records the basic route of the buckwheat grain. Once the buckwheat is harvested, it may or may not be hulled before grinding. In Japan and some European countries the hull is removed before the grain is ground. In North America, however, the hull is ground together with the soft, inner kernel and only later is it sifted out. The latter method may be more economical, but also accounts for a slight bitterness in the final product.

when virtually "running for a living," made use of a simple straw sandal with no heel, illuminating the benefit of both of these eminently serviceable items.

About two weeks after seeding, a sprout will normally grow to 6 to 10 inches, and sometimes 12 inches, in height. Once buckwheat has sprouted, it continues to grow day and night. Ordinarily, plants stop growing at night, but buckwheat utilizes energy and nutrition stored during the day to grow through the night.

This is one reason that "a big difference between day and night temperatures" is a key factor to obtaining superior quality of buckwheat. It implies that if the temperature at night becomes sufficiently cool without freezing, buckwheat's propensity to "burn up its excess energy" will be suppressed.

After approximately one month, clusters, or corollas, of flowers begin to appear. Even as the flowers open, the plant continues to grow. In other words, unlike most other plant life, buckwheat's nutritional and reproductive cycles occur simultaneously.

The flowers open up and form seeds along the whole of the branch, blooming from bottom to top, continuously over a number of days. Likewise, the corresponding seeds fertilize and mature at different times. After 30 days, as many as 625 flowers may be counted on a single stem. In its early stages, the seed is a beautiful dark red color. This stage has been likened to the warm glow of an old lamp: "The fire [buckwheat kernel] within the lantern [flower] is lit." As the seeds mature, they become darker still. When they reach maturity, they fall easily from their branch with only the slightest waving of the hand. This is a characteristic common among wild plants, seemingly adding credence to the opinion that the wild variety of buckwheat was the original from which the common variety evolved. Therefore, when about 70 percent of the seeds *start* to change from red to dark brown, the whole field is harvested.

After harvesting, branches of buckwheat are hung upside down tepee-style to dry in the sun for about three to seven days. This is because, as the adage "It takes three days for buckwheat to realize it has been harvested" implies, buckwheat should be treated with care, as if it is still growing. This time period allows the seed to mature, and it is said that the final product will be superior.

The buckwheat is then threshed and allowed to dry further in the wind and sun. If these two factors are sufficiently strong, good-quality buckwheat can be expected.

Recently, with the advances in technology, a combine that can harvest and thresh the buckwheat in the same step has come into use. In this case, the seed is sufficiently dried with only one week of sunshine. Also, in some cases, the buckwheat is then carried to a drying factory where a temperature-controlled wind-blowing machine is employed. Traditional millers in Japan believe that the temperatures used during the drying process should never exceed 82°F, instead of the 86°F plus often employed in America and Canada.

If less than ideal conditions are applied (say, in the event that the grain is put into a drying machine too soon), professional millers claim that a noticeable decrease in quality and freshness, which inevitably affect the taste, fragrance, and color of the buckwheat, can be detected. Why this occurs is not known but one hypothesis put forth postulates a chemical reaction between the fat and chlorophyll in buckwheat since the kernel is still alive and growing at this stage.

Next, the harvested grain is sent to the millers, whose task it is to turn the buckwheat into flour and groats while retaining the natural sweetness of the ripened grain.

The seed has four basic components: the outer shell (or hull), the seed coat, the endosperm tissue, and the embryo. The taste, texture, color, and fragrance exhibited by the buckwheat flour are largely determined according to how the seed is ground and sifted after the outer shell is removed. That is, the buckwheat grain will yield different varieties of buckwheat flour, according to the degree of sifting and, later, the ratios in which the four distinct sections are combined.

There are basically three steps in the hulling process. The first is to remove the dust, soil, and other grit that may still be clinging to the

A Cross Section of the Buckwheat Seed

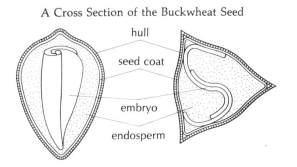

grains, and then sort the kernels according to size. The second step is to remove the hard outer shells either by steaming (for fifteen minutes and then removing the hulls, producing "kasha") or by cracking the outer crushed hulls in a preliminary grinding process, and then removing the hulls after the milling by sifting. Although step one is easy enough to accomplish, the task of removing the outer shells completely without cracking the kernels is extremely difficult. In step three, the hulled kernels are ground together and then sifted several times. The sifting continues until most of the remaining bits of hull is removed.

In Japan, where soba noodles and other dishes have developed a strong following, the flour-making process has been honed to something resembling an art (like so much else in Japan). As such, an in-depth examination of the miller's techniques may prove invaluable not only for millers and farmers outside Japan but for discerning cooks and those concerned with nutrition.

Buckwheat that is to be ground that day is taken out of the storage room, where it is kept at a constant 59°F, and put into a machine that will separate the buckwheat from the little twigs, sand, and other debris that inevitably accumulates during the harvesting. At the same time the hulls are cleaned and polished.

The whole buckwheat is next poured into a machine which separates the buckwheat according to size—large, medium, or small. This is done by a sifting machine which utilizes a series of three progressively smaller-meshed screens.

The whole buckwheat is now put through a preliminary grinder to crack the outer protective hull: first the large-, then the medium-, and finally the small-sized kernels.

The coarsely ground grain then travels through a second type of vibrating sifter that separates the cracked grain into three basic groups: material from the seed coat, spermoderm (with a larger and smaller percentage of hulls), and the flour from the embryo/endosperm derived from the centermost part of the buckwheat.

Although the flour from the last category is now ready for the final grinding, flour in the first two groups must pass through the preliminary stages several times. Each time a bit more of the hulls is removed. Finally, a fan-type blower is employed to separate the flour from the heavier hull material.

The cracked grain is now ready to be ground into a fine flour. There are basically two different systems for milling buckwheat: the roll method, which utilizes steel rollers, and the stone-ground method. The advantage of the former is that it is capable of producing a large quantity of flour quickly, lowering the price. Yet, since heat easily affects the quality of buckwheat, it is important not to allow the steel rollers to become too hot. The latter method is considered the ideal way of milling buckwheat because the millstones are carefully controlled to rotate only about 15 to 18 times per minute. In addition the amount that enters the millstones with each rotation is also regulated. The result is a flour which yields more viscosity during the noodle-making process, thus making it easier to obtain a successful result. However, millstones—hand-turned or electric—can grind only a fraction of what a metal-roll grinder is able to produce in the same amount of time. In olden times, the formidable weight of the heavy stone was either turned by hand or, in the case of a much larger stone, by water power. Nowadays there are electrically powered stone and roll grinding systems available that can be used even by the novice with all of the above factors basically worked out.

Although in reality it is impossible to separate and isolate each section completely, in Japan flour from the center of the kernel (referred to as No. 1 flour) makes up about 25 percent, flour from the endosperm (No. 2) 35 percent, and flour from the seed coat (No. 3) 30 percent. Some factories even make a special flour, known as *uchiko*, for sprinkling on the cutting board and raw noodles to prevent sticking. The remaining 10 percent is made from that part of the buckwheat too close to the shell, called No. 4 (*sanago*). The fourth grade contains a lot of the fiber and roughage and is used to make dry noodles. Some factories even produce fifth, sixth, and seventh grades. Grades 5 through 7 contain some of the outer shell and other valuable water-soluble protein, but are usually discarded, as they are difficult to work into a kneadable dough.

(Interestingly enough, it is said that, after World War II, geisha found a practical use for discarded No. 5 flour. At a time when not only food but other basics such as soap and cosmetics were in short supply, the geisha would wrap the flour in damp cloths and rub their skins to maintain their nice, smooth complexions. They were using the valuable water-soluble proteins, which that part of buckwheat contains in such abundance.)

From the specialist's point of view, the flour from the center (or endosperm tissue) of the kernel is pure white and boasts a figure of more than 1,800 B.U. of pure starch. Noting that representative varieties of wheat contain anywhere from 470 to 925 B.U., buckwheat's superiority becomes evident. It is due to the high viscosity of this starch that buckwheat noodles attain their elasticity and firmness.

After pure-white flour became available, another dimension to soba cuisine was added. Freed from the standard flour's chocolate-brown color, soba cooks began experimenting with natural coloring and flavoring agents such as fragrant citrus rind, green *shiso* leaves, black sesame seeds, red ginger, and even cherry blossoms (see Flavored Soba Noodles). This refinement appealed greatly to the aristocrats and thus the white noodles today are appropriately nicknamed *Gozen Soba*, or buckwheat noodles to be "served before nobles."

Although these early connoisseurs may have found the white noodles more pleasing to the palate, the part of the grain nearest the seed coat contains a considerable amount of buckwheat's protein (34 to 35 percent of the whole). Chocolate brown in color, this section contains little of the viscous starch that is present in the endosperm section, so making noodles from its flour is difficult indeed. Working to produce cohesion, however, are water-soluble proteins such as albumin and globulin. These proteins combine with water in the initial stages of mixing and produce a vitally important stickiness within the dough. In addition, wheat flour is added to ensure proper cohesiveness. Today, noodles made exclusively from this darker flour are called "country soba" (see also "Silk Cut" Soba). They are cut more thickly than regular soba noodles and are appreciated for their sweeter taste and chewiness.

THE FUTURE

Just as the soba chef continues to roll out the noodles and the miller strives to attain an ever-more-refined buckwheat flour (with as little of the hull as possible), the breeders continue to search for a stronger and more productive strain of buckwheat.

As discussed in the History section, buckwheat does not lend itself to improvement through breeding. Even so, researchers have made some steady progress. "In 1955, the cereal crops division of the Canadian Department of Agriculture released the variety Tokyo which originally consisted of a combination of two high-yielding lines selected from a Japanese introduction. The Experimental Farm at Fredericton, New Brunswick, released the Tartary buckwheat variety Welsford in 1947 for use in the Maritime provinces (McGregor)" (De Jong).

Epoch-making announcements were made at both Miyazaki and Shinshu universities in Japan in 1984. The agriculture departments of each of these universities succeeded virtually simultaneously in developing a buckwheat with a seed four times larger than standard size. As their registered names Miyazaki Ootsubu (Miyazaki Large Seeds) and Shin Daigata 4-bai-tai (Shinshu University's Quadruple-sized Type) imply, they are not only bigger but of course of greater weight. In comparison to standard buckwheat ranging from 20 to 34 grams per 100 kernels, they weigh in at 40 to 48 grams. Moreover, the plant stem does not break easily, and therefore it can withstand the pressures of machine harvesting, thereby increasing yield potential. And most important, its taste is said to be every bit as good as original buckwheat's.

Furthermore, since an increase in the quantity of the harvest has also been reported, a more profitable yield seems quite possible in the future. Further, Professor Akio Ujihara announced in December of 1987 the successful cross-pollination of the wild buckwheat (*F. cymosum*) from Nepal and common buckwheat (*F. esculentum*). The hope is that the new plant will be able to self-pollinate like its wild parent, and at the same time produce a seed that will cling tightly to the branch so that it can be harvested more easily, thereby increasing the overall yield.

Experiments like these provide hope, and farmers worldwide might be persuaded to plant buckwheat in fields that have until now been used almost exclusively for rice cultivation. These new developments are also attracting great attention from scientists around the world and may eventually help the situation of world production at large.

Through the lineage of great botanists like Hunt, Coe, and Kellog, to modern-day specialists like Campbell, Kreft, Javornik, and others in the West, as well as from Sugawara, Nagatomo, Ujihara, Adachi, and other well-respected botanists in the East, the search, study, and experimentation continues and East is meeting West.

# History

Buckwheat has always been a food for the people. In Eastern Europe it remains an essential staple in the daily diet and has held a respectable place in Western European cooking as well. Tracing the dissemination of buckwheat throughout the world and the subsequent development of a full-fledged soba cuisine in Japan has proved illuminating. Not only does it provide a fascinating look at the life and habits of an earlier time, it underscores buckwheat's vital role as an important food source as early as the fifteenth century in Europe and A.D. 800 in Japan.

## THE DISSEMINATION OF BUCKWHEAT

There are many theories concerning buckwheat's name and place of origin. Modern-day crop evolution specialist and professor of plant genetics (at the University of Illinois, Urbana) Jack R. Harlan warns that "the idea of a center—an area in which things originate and out of which things are dispersed—is reasonable, logical, and intellectually satisfying, but it does not always agree with the evidence." Harlan believes that "agriculture may originate in discrete centers or evolve over vast areas without definable centers." In other words, buckwheat may have evolved in several places simultaneously.

Nevertheless, as early as the middle of the last century scientists had began speculating on buckwheat's birthplace. The Swiss botanist Alphonse de Candolle, in his book *The Origins of Cultivated Plants* (1881), maintained that it was near Lake Baikal or the valley-basin of the Amal River in Siberia, and yet he cautioned that "it is hard to define the limit of the wild plant [the perennial species, *F. cymosum*, the probable ultimate source of both common and Tartary buckwheat] on (*sic*) the confines of Europe and Asia, in the Himalayas, because the nearer we approach its original country, the more often buckwheat escapes from cultivation and becomes quasi-wild. In Japan these semi-naturalizations are not rare." In the 1940s and 1950s other scientists placed the center of origin in the Manchurian region. These ideas represent what is referred to as the Northern Theory.

The Southern Theory centering on China was proposed in the 1930s by the world-renowned Russian botanist N. I. Vaviloff. Harlan wrote of the man and his work: "For nearly half a century the charisma of the man himself and the elegant simplicity of his methodology have dominated theories and concepts about the origin of plants." In his "Botanical-Geographic Principles of Selection" (1935), Vaviloff stated that "the earliest and largest independent center of the world's agriculture and of the origin of cultivated plants consists of the mountainous region of central and western China, together with the adjacent lowlands." Included on the list of "Cereals and Other Grains" along with soybeans, adzuki beans, and millet were buckwheat (*F. esculentum moench*) and Tartar buckwheat (*F. tataricum gaertn*). Yet "in Vaviloff's time it was not possible to predict the enormous support that archaeology in general and archaeobotany in particular could give studies of the origin of cultivated plants and the emergence of agriculture. . . . The modern approach is more in the tradition of de Candolle than Vaviloff, in that it attempts to integrate all sources of information" (Harlan). Yet, recent analysis of buckwheat-seed remains excavated from sites in Hokkaido, Kyoto, and other areas has lent further credibility to the Southern Theory, and today it is the most widely accepted of the two. Specifically, the area of Unnan State in southern China is considered a likely candidate for buckwheat's place of origin.

Others claimed the areas in and around Tibet and the Himalayan mountains of either western China or northern India to be the site of buckwheat's beginnings.

Thomas Hunt, a professor of agronomy, wrote in 1914 that "although buckwheat is known to have been cultivated in China for 1,000 years (before coming to Europe), it is not believed to be very ancient, being 'unknown to the ancient Egyptians, Greeks, and Romans.' The first written records are Chinese scripts of the fifth and sixth centuries."

From southern China, buckwheat is believed to have spread in all directions: westward to Nepal, northern India, and Bhutan; and north and east to the rest of China, Russia, and Korea.

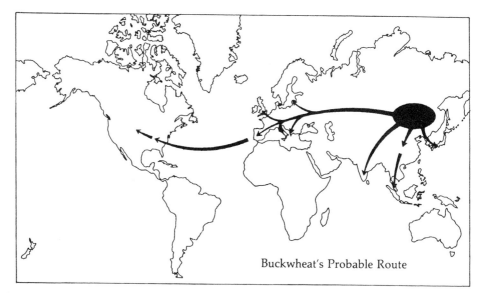

Buckwheat's Probable Route

Buckwheat came to Europe and America by traveling westward from its center of origin. De Candolle believed that the plant first entered Europe during the Middles Ages through Tartary and Russia. It probably passed through the lands of the Saracens, the nomadic Arabic peoples inhabiting the deserts between Syria and Arabia, for it later came to be widely known in French as *blé sarrasin* (Saracen wheat). Other opinions hold that returning Crusaders brought back buckwheat from this area to Europe in the twelfth century. The Oxford English Dictionary (1933) states that "buckwheat was introduced into Europe by the Turks about the thirteenth century," while researchers Hughes and Henson (1934) mention it "reaching Germany early in the 15th century."

The earliest known reference to its cultivation in Germany appeared in the Mecklenburgh register of 1436. It began to be widely cultivated in Russia during the 1400s, and during the 1500s it "spread toward the center of Europe and was cultivated for several centuries in England, France, Spain, Italy, Germany, and Russia. It also found a place in the agriculture of Africa and Brazil" (Campbell). The earliest English-language reference in the Oxford English Dictionary is by Turner in 1548.

Dutch colonists who settled along the Hudson River in what is now New York City brought buckwheat to America. In the 1800s it became popular in the South as an inexpensive flour source, and by 1866 an impressive 22 million bushels a year were being produced, primarily in New York and Pennsylvania. "Unlike the true cereal grains such as wheat, oats, and rye, it may be grown with abundant yields on poor, thin, arid soil where the climate is cool and moist" (Coe). The favorite use was in pancakes. This fare became so popular it found its way into Stephen Foster's famous song "Oh, Susanna" of 1846:

> De buckwheat cake was in her mouth
> De tear was in her eye
> Says I: "I'm coming from de South"
> Susanna, don't you cry.

In fact, buckwheat cakes made from fresh flour even rated a mention in an 1882 magazine, *Garden*: "To go to America for a good . . . buckwheat cake" (OED).

Thereafter production began a long, slow decline. Several factors were responsible, including a decrease in the demand for buckwheat flour and for feed, the difficulty in developing new strains to improve crop yield, and advances in agricultural techniques that increased the yields of other crops on marginal farm land, nominally buckwheat's domain.

"In common with other countries, the acreage under buckwheat in Canada declined steadily until the early 1960s, but has increased since then as a result of demand for export, mainly to Japan. Since 1967, more than 50 percent of the total Canadian production has been centered in Manitoba. The yield per acre has fluctuated considerably, probably as a result of the susceptibility of the crop to such weather conditions as frost and drought. There has been no apparent increase in yield per acre in Manitoba over the last 25 years. Furthermore, Leighty has reported that over the period 1909–1913, the average yield in Canada was about 23–24 bushels/acre. Thus there appears to have been little or no increase in yield over the last 50 years and modern agricultural technology seems not so far to have made any significant impact on the crop" (De Jong).

Today, the Soviet Union and China are by far the world's leading producers of buckwheat, followed by France, Poland, Canada, and the United States.

BUCKWHEAT REACHES JAPAN

Up until quite recently, with only scant references in historical documents to go by, scientists believed buckwheat to have entered southern Japan from Korean via the island of Tsushima around or before the early part of the seventh century.

With the development of more modern methods of investigation such as pollen analysis, however, historians have received new fuel for consideration. Utilizing this technique, scientists in Japan were able to analyze ancient buckwheat pollen found among excavated remains dating back to the Jomon period (10,000 B.C.–300 B.C.) in the northernmost island of Hokkaido and in other areas of Japan as well. With discoveries like these, historians understandably differ as to exactly when and by which route buckwheat found its way to Japan.

Its earliest appearance in extant written records is not a matter of conjecture, however. The word *buckwheat* first appears in historical documents dated 722, in one of six historical logs covering the period from 697 to 791, in the reign of the empress Gensho. It was a trying time, and the empress issued the following proclamation to local leaders: "It is now summer and there is no rain. Rice has been planted but is not growing. The possibility of famine looms. I command the officials to encourage the cultivation of buckwheat and barley and to set up warehouses in order to store the food harvested." Even then buckwheat's value as a quick-growing, highly nutritious food was understood, and monarchs relied on it in times when the more profitable rice crop failed them.

Known for its ability to grow even in barren soil and to go from seed to grain in the relatively short period of 75 days, buckwheat played an indispensable role as a crop that could help offset the effects of poor harvests and the dangers of famine. Due to primitive methods of cultivation, poor weather, and frequent states of war during these early times, rice was an extremely limited and precious commodity. Even when there was a decent harvest, the farmers were more inclined to use it as a form of payment of tax. Thus, buckwheat became a supplementary food along with wheat, millet, and barnyard grasses.

By the Kamakura period (1185–1333), buckwheat had become more widely available and is thought to have been eaten either as a whole grain in the form of gruels and porridges, or ground roughly into flour and used in a manner similar to wheat, millet, and other grains.

Gradually, cooking styles highlighting buckwheat's own unique character began to appear. Simple, filling foods like buckwheat dumplings developed. Variations on this dish sprang up across the country. Sweetened bean pastes or cooked vegetables, such as pumpkins, turnips, and potatoes, were stuffed into the centers of the dumplings. These were then steamed, baked, fried, or roasted to make primitive muffins and pastries.

Until the late sixteenth century, dumpling cooking in its numerous forms was the mainstay of buckwheat cooking. It is said that the shogun Hideyoshi Toyotomi, virtual ruler of Japan from 1588 to 1595 and a stout supporter of the tea ceremony, also had a great liking for the soba dumpling.

Just when and where soba noodles came into being is unclear, but hints can be gleaned from various documents, diaries, and other ancient literature. Generally, most Japanese culinary historians agree that soba noodles were probably first made in the confines of the temples and later spread to the general populace. This is a reasonable assumption since priests in those days traveled to China, the birthplace of the noodle, for training and in addition received guests from abroad. The oldest extant writings mentioning buckwheat noodles, or *soba-kiri*, are said to be the diaries of the priest Jisho. In an entry dated February 3, 1614, he noted that "we were served buckwheat noodles at the Jomyo Temple" in Edo (Tokyo). In those days, only the wealthy people could afford to provide formal or decent burial grounds for their kin. As such, the less fortunate were often forced to just abandon or bury their deceased in desolate mountain areas. Therefore, many of the common people would pay their respects at local temples instead. Jomyo Temple priests would offer temple guests a bowl of soba. Amusingly, and as so often happens, as

A prototypical soba shop in the Shijogawara pleasure quarter of Kyoto. Note the long rolling pin still used by professional soba makers today. Artist unknown. *Nihonga*, ca. 1635.

word spread about the free service of these very satisfying noodles, people began to flock to this temple in large numbers. Eventually, the priests became annoyed at having to spend so much time meeting the demand and discontinued the service altogether.

Jisho's entry reveals no sense of surprise or novelty concerning the soba noodles. This suggests that they were no longer a new idea. So the question remains as to how far back the custom of soba noodles reaches. Since another work by the priest Genkei in the early Muromachi period (1394–1596) only mentions *udon* (thick wheat noodles) and *somen* noodles, the date can be approximated if not pinpointed. The modern-day buckwheat historian Shigeru Niijima places their development somewhere between 1596 and 1614.

The exact location of their origin is also open for debate. One book published in the Genroku period (1688–1704) cites the Seiun Temple (located near present-day Kofu, in Yamanashi Prefecture, 70 miles from central Tokyo), while another book, written about ten years later, gives the area around Kiso, Nagano Prefecture (previously Motoyama), the nod. Neither of these accounts claims to be indisputable, however, being only the result of hearsay. Furthermore, by modern standards, these two places are less than an hour's train ride apart.

In any event, without being too far off, it is assumed that the techniques involved in making udon and somen, introduced from China to Japan during the Heian period (794–1185), eventually led to the development of soba noodles in Japan some four hundred years ago in the Yamanashi-Nagano region.

Some support for the above theory can be found in a light verse composed by a popular humorist of the Edo period (1600–1868) by the name of Shokusanjin (1749–1823). While visiting the popular resort area of Motoyama, he wrote the following play on words:

| | |
|---|---|
| Everybody knows | *Motoyama no* |
| how famous Motoyama is for | *Soba meibutsu to* |
| buckwheat noodles. | *Tare mo shiru* |
| Here the luggage is | *Nimotsu wa koko ni* |
| put down/grated radish. | *Oroshi daikon* |

By tacking on the word *daikon* (radish) at the very end, he puns on the word *oroshi* (meaning both to "put something down" or "grate a vegetable"), changing the meaning from "Here the luggage is put down" to "Here the luggage is grated radish," a popular condiment for soba noodles.

The important point is simply that the area had already developed a reputation for its soba noodles, lending further credence to the Yamanashi-Nagano theory.

THE RISE OF SOBA

During the years between 1596 and 1614, laborers and cooks poured in from all over the country to help with the development of the new capital city, Edo, under the new shogun, Ieyasu Tokugawa. It was during this time that soba noodles sprang into great popularity. In addition to being a food the laborers could afford, it provided a quick energy source both at lunchtime and at the end of a long, hard day of work. (Interestingly enough, just as in the pioneer days of the Wild West, three-fourths of the population in Tokyo was said to be male.) Also, soba noodles seemed to fit the personality of the people like a glove. This is clearly reflected by the following verse attributed to the famous haiku poet Basho (1644–94): "Haiku and soba match the spirit of Tokyo."

In 1642, the government prohibited the selling of udon, soba, tofu, and similar nutritional staples for profit due to an extremely severe famine. Food was strictly rationed to each family, and meals had to be stretched by adding root plants to these basics.

In 1643, the first book describing the making of soba noodles in detail, *Tales of Cooking* (*Ryori monogatari*), was published. It mentions that buckwheat flour could be kneaded together with plain water, the water discarded during the washing of rice, hot water, or mashed tofu. That is, although taken for granted today, the practice of using wheat as a binding agent had not yet developed.

From the written evidence of several sources, the noodles at these early establishments are thought to have been made without the addition of wheat flour. Furthermore, it is thought that the noodles were most likely steamed instead of boiled. This technique was employed to compensate for the primitive methods of milling that existed at the time. That is, since buckwheat has no gluten of its own and the flour produced back then was quite probably limited in its fineness and elasticity, noodles made from only buckwheat were prone to break into little pieces when boiled. (As buckwheat's protein melts and dissolves in hot water, there is not sufficient binding power to hold the noodles together.) Therefore, by steaming, not only were the noodles not subjected to the rapid movement of boiling water, but what little elasticity the coarse flour did have could be coaxed out to produce a successful noodle.

According to one theory, the idea of combining wheat and buckwheat flours was introduced by the Korean priest Genchin upon his visit to the famous temple Todaiji, sometime between 1624 and 1643. Yet, as other books published as late as 1689 fail to mention wheat as an ingredient in the process, it is thought that this did not become standard practice until at least the early 1700s, and perhaps not even until the mid-1720s. One reason for speculation is that, during this period, wheat was widely available only from late autumn to early spring.

In the rural areas, such local sources as potatoes, burdock leaves, and the young leaves of the buckwheat plant itself served as binding agents to help add strength and elasticity to the mixture. Even today, these variations on the basic soba noodle continue to be made.

In March 1657, as a result of the disastrous Furisode Fire, the economy of Tokyo suffered a severe setback. Over two-thirds of the city was destroyed in the two-day conflagrations, and more than 100,000 perished in it or the snowstorm that hit the city on the following day.

Within four or five years, however, the city was reported to have been completely rebuilt, and in 1664 the government permitted the selling of food (buckwheat noodles included) in public again.

The book *Morisada Manko* (1853), a record of the customs of the Edo period, indirectly confirms the last point. The author wrote, "In 1664, *kendon* buckwheat noodles [explained below] appeared, but as yet were eaten only by the ordinary people, not being deemed fit for the noble classes." From this statement two things can be surmised. One, of course, is that the crucial period of adversity caused by famine and fire had subsided. The other is that, not only were the noodle dishes themselves of low quality, but the shops that sold them, set up to cater to the laborers and commoners, quite probably were centered in the "downtown" section of town. Thus, unlike the soba shops of today, the interiors were probably very sparse, functional affairs at best.

By taking a look at the names of two prototypical soba dishes (reported to have appeared as early as the period 1624–44), it becomes clear that in the early stages soba noodles appealed mainly to the laborers and lower classes. One dish, called "honest soba" (*shojiki soba*), was sold around the grounds of the Sensoji temple in Asakusa, and the other, "horseman's soba" (*umakatta soba*), was popular in the area around Denma in Yotsuya.

The first dish received its name from its close association with the temples, where honesty was the guiding rule of conduct. The latter was coined for people who had the taxing job of walking ahead of the horse and pulling its reins for the purpose of guiding aristocrats or delivering parcels to their proper destination. This was a popular means of getting from station to station during this period, and the horseman's service was in great demand. Walking long distances every day, their need for a good and cheap energy supply can easily be imagined. The area around Denma in Yotsuya became a regular stop, a place where horsemen could "fuel up" by eating soba. They constituted such a steady clientele that the soba was named for them.

The reference to *kendon* soba in the earlier passage adds another dimension. First of all, let it be said that the word *kendon* connotes a coarse or loud manner of speech or activity. Next, during this period, the red-light district of Yoshiwara was in its initial stages. Various ranks of professional entertainers existed, according to their education and talent. Although extremely difficult to achieve, the highest rank conferred was that of *tayu*. This position was achieved only with great difficulty: Women had to be proficient in poetry, the classics, calligraphy, and other arts, as well as be adept at the tea ceremony. Obviously, those who could qualify were so few in number that they could demand almost any price, and of course associated with only the very rich or those who had the same level of education. On the other end of the scale were those who lacked any education whatsoever. Virtually held hostage within the confines of their respective shops, they would call out to passers-by in a loud voice, following this with no more than foolish chatter after services were rendered. Being at first loud and noisy, but later dull and boring, they became known as "kendon girls."

In the same period, many soba shops offering only the lowest and cheapest quality food also tried to draw customers to their shops by calling out in a loud voice. Once in the shop, however, the customers found the place totally lacking in etiquette: The shop's service come to an abrupt end when the customer's order was slapped down on the counter in a quick, rough manner. Sure enough, their fare was soon tagged with the unbecoming name "kendon soba."

## SOBA OVERTAKES UDON

Before 1690, shops specializing exclusively in soba were rare. Generally, soba noodles were sold at udon restaurants and regular restaurants featuring rice dishes as a way to expand the menu, and at confectionery shops as an additional source of income.

Up until this time, udon was the mainstay of "Japanese pasta," and soba was still in its infancy. Gradually, however, shops specializing in soba came into their own and soon greatly outnumbered their predecessors. This situation is vividly depicted by the famous *ukiyo-e* artist Moronobu Hishikawa in his *Tokaido no bunken ezu* (*The Area Around Tokaido Station*) in 1690. Signboards for soba shops outnumber their udon/soba competitors twenty-one to six, and only one sign features udon/somen.

Soba shops were coming into their own, so much so that they began to appear in contemporary popular stories and legends. The year 1703 saw the culmination of the saga of the 47 *ronin*, or masterless samurai, one of the most celebrated incidents of perseverance and loyalty in Japanese history. On the night before the consummation of their two-year plan to revenge the wrongful treatment and consequent death of their lord, the 47 loyal retainers are said to have gathered on the second floor of a soba shop. Whether or not they actually met at a soba shop is questionable; yet, the fact that stories and Kabuki plays written about this true tale portray it as being so at least indicates how pervasive soba shops had become.

Sometime between 1711 and 1726, the forerunner of today's *Kake Soba*, or Hot Soba Noodles in a Broth, is said to have appeared at the restaurant Shinano in Tokyo. Interestingly enough, unlike the hot version of today, it is reported that room-temperature or cool soup broth was poured over the cooked noodles. Laborers came in for a quick bowl of noodles and preferred to down them as quickly as possible. It can be imagined how waiting for the broth to be heated would have been a source of irritation. The expression "Arguments and fire are what Tokyo

Central section of a humorous print of the 47 *ronin*. Three retainers eagerly devour bowls of soba, foreshadowing their final rendezvous in a soba shop. Hiroshige Ando. *Ukiyo-e* (detail), ca. 1830.

is known for" during this period accurately reflects the temperament of the times and certainly seems to lend credibility to this idea.

In 1728, an article published in a book dealing with the clothing, food, and daily life of the times stated that by 1726 the advertising board TWO-EIGHT INSTANT KENDON SOBA had appeared in the Kanda area of Tokyo. That it was a variation of the basic kendon soba is certain, but what was the meaning of *two-eight* and *instant*?

Concerning the former, various explanations have been put forth, one being that *two-eight* signifies the ratio of wheat flour to buckwheat flour (that is, two parts wheat flour to eight parts buckwheat). Another possibility concerns the price of the soba itself. The currency of the time was *mon* instead of the yen of today. Therefore, the term *two-eight* is thought to have stood for two portions of soba at eight mon each, a price considered to be well within the means of the laborers. Both of these interpretations, as well as others, are still a matter of speculation today.

The word *instant* in the signboard is worth a bit more reflection. If allowed to sit for a while after rolling out and cutting, soba made from 100-percent buckwheat is prone to dry up and hence break into small pieces when cooked, even if it is carefully steamed. To prevent this from happening, the noodles are thus rolled and cut fresh upon order, obviously requiring the customer to wait. Thus, the concept of "instant" soba would not have been possible. However, if wheat is added to the process the noodle will hold together, due to the wheat's gluten. Thus, soba noodles can be made in advance, "cooked instantly" or even precooked, and simply reheated, as many of today's fast-food noodle stands do. This, then, is thought to be the real significance of the TWO-EIGHT INSTANT KENDON SOBA signboard: The technique of blending wheat flour with the buckwheat had finally become a standard practice.

THE EMERGENCE OF A SOBA CUISINE
Edo-period culture reached its peak during the period 1751 to 1801. And gradually, the increased level of extravagance started to create a period of decadence, said to have occurred between 1804 and 1830. Soba shops were greatly affected.

Originally considered a food for the working class, soba cuisine slowly evolved in more sophisticated establishments that were now frequently visited by the aristocrats.

From around 1789, the shops started to be redecorated with gorgeous *tatami* interiors resembling those of elegant teahouses, and began to

Humorous depiction of farmers celebrating a successful harvest with soba.

offer saké. Also at about this time, the restaurant Nagasaka, located in Azabu near Roppongi, started to feature the highly refined pure-white—and subsequently different-colored and -flavored—buckwheat noodles, in addition to the standard type.

Utensils became more refined as well. Exquisitely worked soba utensils—serving trays, porcelain, and so on—appeared which, if made today, would demand phenomenal prices. One of the most representative pieces of the era is the *Lacquered Kendon Box* owned for a time by the writer Takizawa Bakin. Considered a masterpiece of craftsmanship, it is an exquisitely lacquered black box with a shiny shell-type design painted on the outside. More than just your average container, it made a great impression on the lords and aristocrats visiting the soba establishments where it was displayed. It is recorded that this piece was part of an antique exhibition during the early 1800s. Even today, it can be seen at museums exhibiting the works of the Edo period.

By 1818, there were said to have been over 6,000 noodle shops in Edo, with soba shops making up about half of this total. It was reported that you couldn't walk more than 150 yards in any direction without running into at least one soba shop.

In direct contrast to the growing sophistication of the high-class restaurants, the low-class shops, now commonly referred to as "two-eight" shops, sank even lower. Eventually this earned them the reputation of serving "junk-food" soba (*da-soba*). To further distinguish their establishments from lesser shops, the masters of the better shops began to post signs such as HANDMADE (*te-uchi*) or ONE-HUNDRED PERCENT SOBA (*ki-soba*) in front of their shops. Imagine the wit of putting out a sign reading HANDMADE in an age when noodle machines had not yet come into being. Of course everything was still being made by hand, but the intended meaning was "We are selling soba that is skillfully made from high-quality ingredients—not junk food."

Near the end of the Edo period, the two-eight shops began to imitate the high-class shops by upgrading their decor and exteriors. Some even went so far as to put out the same HANDMADE signs in front of their stores. Gradually it became difficult to distinguish one from the other, thus marking the beginning of the situation that exists today. Unless tipped off and led to such a shop by a friend, it became impossible to detect from the outside which shop was really serving high-quality, handmade soba.

According to the previously mentioned book *Morisada Manko*, around 1860 there was an official meeting of soba-shop proprietors concerning the standardizing of prices. Over 3,700 soba shops were on the register for this meeting (although the actual number of soba shops must have been far greater). Today, although the population of Tokyo is more than ten times what it was during the late Edo period, the number of soba shops has only doubled.

## NIGHTHAWK, WIND-CHIME, AND NIGHT-STAND SOBA

In the evenings the street stalls began to sell hot soba noodles in a hearty broth meant to cut the evening chill. It is not clear when they first began, but as a perusal of old government notices reveals that they were temporarily prohibited in 1686 due to the outbreak of numerous fires (a result of careless operators), it is evident that they existed before that time.

As the hawk is also active late into the night, the nickname *yotaka-soba* ("nighthawk soba") was soon appended to the stalls. Yet another contributing factor is said to have been that these establishments were often frequented by streetwalkers out looking for customers. Although this kind of activity was officially restricted to the confines of Yoshiwara, there were those who dared to solicit elsewhere. Upon calling out to a potential customer, they would say *"Chotto, chotto"* ("Just a minute. . . ."), which somewhat resembled the hawk's cry, "cho, cho." True or not, the nickname stuck. In any event, both the nighttime stall operators and the street professionals received the nickname "nighthawk" for their nocturnal habits.

A short lyric-like verse (*senryu*) penned around this period plays on, among other things, these two nighthawks.

> Two customers                *Kyaku futatsu*
> woman's work done            *Tsubushite yotaka*
> brings three helpings of soba.  *Mitsu kui*

Two nighthawkers. A kabuki scene. Utagawa Toyokuni I. *Ukiyo-e*, ca. 1816.

Both in Tokyo and Osaka, people of respectability began visiting these stands. They were known to approach inconspicuously and order in a soft voice. Although it is probably true that they didn't want to disturb or awaken the neighborhood people (who lived in dwellings literally constructed of thin wood and paper walls and who, in addition, customarily rose and set with the sun, due to the expense of oil lighting and heating), it is not unreasonable to assume that they wanted to avoid any association with the seedier aspects of the business.

In order to encourage well-heeled visitors and remain concurrent with their udon cousins, soba operators in Tokyo began to upgrade their stalls. They struck upon the idea of using the delicate sound of a wind chime to lure customers. Other inducements, including charming bowls and a wide selection of choice garnishes, were added as well. Appropriately enough, these stalls became known as "wind-chime soba" stands and were a tremendous hit.

Not to be outdone by the success of their rivals, the nighthawk sellers also started to attach wind chimes to their stands. In response, the original wind-chime stands began calling out to the customers. Once again, it became virtually impossible to distinguish between the styles.

From 1804 to 1830, the number of soba shops offering good quality fare at reasonable prices began to increase. As a result of this and the extravagance of the age, the image and popularity of the night stands began to wane. Gradually they were by and large forced out of business.

The shogunate's control over Edo and the rest of Japan began to decline toward the end of the Edo period. Where once strict punishment was meted out for any critical stance taken toward the ruling class, near the end indirect ridicule became the order of the day. In this print a samurai falls victim to a dog and a tray of soba. Utagawa Hirokage. *Ukiyo-e* (detail), 1859.

SOBA FROM 1868 TO THE PRESENT

The buckwheat available in Tokyo during the Meiji period (1868–1912) came primarily by one of two routes: what are known as the mountain route and the river route. Buckwheat from the former was transported by horse from the mountainous areas of Nerima and Jindaiji, northwest of Tokyo, or from the Fujisawa area, southwest of Tokyo. Ground mainly in the Shinjuku and Hodogaya areas, the flour was then distributed among the stores of Tokyo. The Ishimori flour factory in Nakano (near Shinjuku) and the Kitagawa flour factory in Hodogaya trace their roots back to this period.

However, with the moving of the imperial capital to Tokyo, this supply was insufficient in and of itself. Therefore, increasingly larger quantities of buckwheat were shipped in from country areas to satisfy demand. Unfortunately, after undergoing such long storage under moist conditions, this latter buckwheat was thought to be considerably inferior.

In the early stages, the buckwheat was turned into flour utilizing man-powered millstones 21 inches (one *chokei*) in width. At about the time of the war between Japan and China in 1894–95, oil engines began to be employed. Nowadays, mainly steel roll grinders from Europe are used, in addition to the few millstones still employed to provide high-quality flour to the traditional "handmade" shops.

In March 1888, with the first patenting of a noodle machine, by a Mr. Shinzaki from the Kyushu region, the long road from handmade to machine-made noodles was bridged.

In 1942, amid World War II, the whole Japanese economy collapsed and, along with the other industries, the restaurant business was completely abandoned. Finally, in 1950, the Japanese economy began to recover and the restaurant industry reestablished itself. It is said that the supply of food in Japan was critical during the war years but actually worse during the six years that followed. Due to the scope of its defeat, it is perhaps unavoidable that attention shifted from things Japanese to Western styles. As a result, not only did the ingredients and techniques of the soba maker suffer a temporary decline in quality, but the consciousness of the people concerning soba's place in the daily diet seemed to have received a mighty blow as well.

With the passage of 40 years, over 40,000 soba shops have sprung back up all over the country. Yet, 80 to 90 percent of these retain only the most superficial resemblance to real soba establishments, content to serve buckwheat noodles that in reality contain as much wheat as they do buckwheat. In all fairness, these can be refreshing and enjoyable. Yet, if the public's conception of buckwheat stops at this level of awareness, an extreme injustice is being done to this worthy, nutritious, and tasty food.

Nowadays, the word *soba* is lumped together along with spaghetti, udon, etc., as just another type of noodle. In fact, if you mention the word *soba* to people under 30, they are likely to think you are referring to ramen (Chinese noodles). Yet, a resurgent breed carries on with the traditional techniques, serving up buckwheat noodles worthy of their name. However, if you are not led by a friend to one of these establishments, you probably will not have the pleasure of tasting the real thing. Hopefully, the list of shops at the end of this book will help to bridge this gap.

At the same time, Japan now produces only 20 percent of the buckwheat it consumes, with the largest supplier being China, followed by Canada, the United States, and Brazil. Wouldn't it be nice if people in the West could pick up the slack, become more aware of the nugget of nutrition that their countries have in abundance, and give life back to buckwheat noodles?

# APPENDICES

# The Soba Dining Experience

Soba is mainly thought of as a food to eat on the run. It is an ideal light lunch or snack because it can be prepared on short notice and is nourishing as well as easily digested. Yet, the better soba shops also attract an evening clientele, and these more discriminating customers are not in such a hurry. On the contrary, they come in search of a quiet place in which to leisurely enjoy solitude or companionship, a flask of saké, and good, honest fare.

*"Saki ni, sake dake dashite morau!"*

("Anyway, to start with, just bring the saké!")

Traditional soba shops provide light fare, which makes a perfect accompaniment (as it turns out) for saké. Granting, of course, that menus vary slightly from shop to shop, one of the standard ways to start is simply to order a glass of cold or hot saké (depending on the season). In the next breath, order a plate of sliced Rolled Omelette (*Tamago-yaki* in Japanese). At first glance, the omelette closely resembles those made at sushi shops. But just one bite is enough to experience the superior broth of the soba master. Not just sweet, this omelette is much juicier and richer. Some restaurants whip up a fresh batch on order, in which case three to five minutes are necessary to receive a steaming serving of thick, juicy slices.

While eating the omelette slices, the saké begins to entice the senses. As the desire to order another flask arises, order the dish called *nuki* along with it. *Nuki* literally means "left out," not indicating at first just what ingredient is omitted. At traditional soba shops, there are two standard types of *nuki*, chicken or duck *nuki* and tempura *nuki*. *Tori-nuki* (chicken) and *kamo-nuki* (duck) refer to bowls of soup which contain fresh and supple pieces of chicken or duck sautéed with sliced Welsh onions. No soba noodles. No soba anything. Then there is *ten-nuki*. This refers to a bowl of soup with only tempura-fried shrimp. Here, too, the soba is missing. The *nuki* serves as a light soup, imparting a hint of flavor to whet the appetite and complement the saké.

Whatever appetizer is served, it is important that it have a clear and decisive taste. The *nuki* broth, which uses regular soy sauce, assuredly falls into this category. As the warmth of the saké begins to relax you, take one swig of the soup, and all trace or memory of saké disappears. But then the soup begins to tease, creating a pleasant, almost haunting thirst that only saké can quench (or so it seems). In other words, it is doing its job as an appetizer, encouraging one to eat, yet leaving room for another few drinks.

Furthermore, if you make it to one of the shops in this book, where the cooks are top-notch, you will greatly appreciate the high-quality oil used for the duck, chicken, or tempura. While staving off hunger and the desire for a richer repast, the *nuki* prepares the palate for another sip of saké and helps set the stage for the soba.

*Nuki* pleases in the same manner as a crafted English sports car. From the outside the car looks stylish and fancy, but on the other hand, it's at first awkward to drive. In the beginning the gears don't mesh, or the clutch doesn't engage, for example, and you are wondering whether this car is worth all the rave it has been accorded. Yet, as you begin to master its idiosyncrasies and become confident enough to take it for a cruise on the highway, you feel for the first time the pleasure and magnificence of the machine that you are driving. The car hugs the road nicely, and the engine sounds great as it is being wound out.

Order another flask of saké.

By the time you have finished the substantial part of the *nuki* dish (that is, the chewy duck or chicken or the crispy fried shrimp), the light, consommélike broth has "absorbed" some of the tempura batter or natural oils of the fowl. Before you know it, a thick and strong-tasting stewlike porridge forms.

Now is the time to add the hot and sweet-tasting cooking water of soba, called *soba-yu* in Japanese, to the remaining broth. *Soba-yu* is not only added for the purpose of diluting the thickened soup: it provides the fragrance of soba. Drop by drop, this soup is very strong and thick. But it is made with precision, embodying the spirit of the shop. This taste is said to be the real taste of Tokyo.

I'll never forget the first meeting I had with Dr. Tsuji (introduced in the Nutrition section). "The mark of good *nuki* is that it retains its sharp taste down to the last drop of this *soba-yu* soup. Never forget to drink *soba-yu* whenever you eat soba. It contains an abundance of buckwheat's water-soluble proteins and B vitamins."

You can't disguise the taste of a *nuki* soup. By adding *soba-yu*, the diluted broth, the quality of the bonito and soy sauce becomes even more obvious. Shops which take pride in their *nuki* generally make soup that by itself is worth the price of the meal.

Needless to say, soba restaurants that offer good *nuki* present a broth (and dipping sauce) of high quality. In Japan, the soup of such and such an area or place is always a popular topic of discussion among soba-lovers. "What is the ratio of ingredients in his soup?"—this question is an indication that the soba-maker is widely acknowledged for more than just the noodles themselves.

The technique of making delicious *nuki* is still alive and indeed experiencing a comeback in popularity. Yet, keep in mind that most of the regular soba shops are more fast-food–oriented and do not offer *nuki*. As it requires technique, experience, and sense, the art of making good *nuki* places the soba shop in an entirely different category.

As George Ohsawa said, "Everything that has a beginning has an end." In many of the more ordinary soba shops today, if you walk in and ask for *nuki*, they will be at a loss to understand you. It would be forgivable if they would just admit that they don't know the meaning of *nuki*. But to reply that "We don't serve that kind of food here" or, after a long discussion among the chefs as to what the customer wants, to bring out plain, hot *kake soba*, thinking that *ten-nuki* means noodles without tempura! *Nuki* is much different from poor-man's soba.

Whenever you are out in the Tokyo area in the early evening hours, whether in a group or alone, visit the shops selected in this book and enjoy the customary *nuki* with saké before or during your order of soba. It will provide a most extraordinary taste experience and add to your appreciation of both soba and saké at the same time.

# Selected Soba Restaurants in Japan

As a well-traveled photographer friend of mine once quipped, "My favorite restaurants are those which serve large portions at low prices." Certainly, many factors come into play when deciding what and where to eat. Other than price, some obvious considerations are the convenience, the environment, and the quality of service of the restaurant. Last, but certainly not least, come the taste and nutritional content of the food. While many restaurant reviews classify and award stars or points to differentiate one shop from another, it cannot be denied that personal preferences will lead to two entirely different reactions to the same place.

Sometimes when you are running around a big city like Tokyo (or New York or Chicago) you want a light but satisfying meal. In Japan, men and women, businessmen and students, young and old alike, satisfy this need by dropping into the nearest soba stand, usually located near or within any train station. There they can get a big bowl of steaming-hot noodles with loads of *wakame*, vegetables, or tempura toppings for little more than $2.00.

Soba stands constitute about 45 percent of the 41,000 soba shops in Japan today; "town shops," featuring machine-made noodles, make up another 45 percent; and the special traditional soba shops that serve handmade noodles account for about 10 percent. While the ingredients used in soba cuisine at any level are basically decided through tradition, differences in the quality and ratios of these ingredients, as well as individual cooking styles and techniques of masters, enable each stand, restaurant, or unique "hideaway" to maintain its own unique and special taste. By taking a look at the two fundamental elements within soba cuisine—the noodle itself and the broth which accompanies it—we can understand precisely the differences which provide the "special" taste featured at each restaurant.

Soba stands (*tachi gui*) serve noodles that contain only 30 to 40 percent buckwheat and are made at a factory with cheaper flour, yet provide a satisfying, quick meal. In all honesty, some of these establishments serve pretty mediocre stuff, but before you dismiss soba as good for nothing but a cheap meal on the run, try another place, this time looking for one a little more upmarket. In fact, I have often heard newcomers to Japan rave that their local stand serves "such a tasty bowl of noodles, all for $2.00!" when actually it is the taste of the soup which keeps them coming back for more. Soup stocks vary from stand to stand, with some producing quite tasty broths. Keep in mind when entering these places that you can order a variety of toppings to go with your noodles. For example, a *kitsune-wakame-tamago* combination (thin deep-fried tofu, *wakame* seaweed, and egg) can be ordered instead of just one ingredient. On the average, the price of a tray of soba is about $1.65 to $2.00; with tempura, $2.00 to $2.50.

Next in number are soba shops that serve machine-made soba in the towns and deliver to your home. I used to rely heavily on these establishments for my daily meals, either dropping by or calling for home delivery. By and large family-managed affairs, each one has its own homey taste and appeal. A great majority display plastic models of soba outside the restaurant, rendering them easily identifiable. The quality is usually considerably higher than that of the soba stands, and the price is accordingly about two to three times greater. They feature soba that has been made either at the factory or on the premises by the master. The noodles contain 50 to 70 percent buckwheat (and 30 to 50 percent wheat), and are much more elastic than the "stand" variety. These long and thin, easily digestible noodles provide a satisfyingly light meal. I was grateful for the soba home-delivery service during those many times when cooking was out of the question. These soba shops employ various methods for the soup stock, using medium- to high-grade ingredients and often using the bonito twice after allowing it to dry. The price of a tray of plain soba is about $2.35 to $2.65; and with tempura, $4.35 to $6.65.

Finally, we come to the traditional handmade-soba restaurants: It is from this group that we have selected the restaurants reviewed here. Traditional soba restaurants constitute less than 10 percent of the whole, or roughly 4,000 restaurants, which is why so few people have ever enjoyed the experience of eating fine soba. At the most traditional of these establishments, the soba noodles are made completely by hand using only a mixing bowl, rolling pin, board, and knife. Others, which deal in a large volume, use a mixing machine in the beginning, and sometimes even a cutting aid is used at the end. Some shops place greater emphasis on the quality of the other ingredients. Of the establishments serving only handmade soba, only about 10 percent follow the adage "First year, mixing; second year, rolling; third year, cutting." Those that do are usually headed by a soba master. Thus, there are perhaps as many as 400 soba masters in Japan today, many of whom have become quite famous, attracting not only a wide clientele but also apprentices, one of whom will be allowed to carry on each shop's name.

However, the differentiation does not end there. We can even say that of these 400 masters, only 10 to 15 percent offer soba flour ground fresh that day. *If you experience soba made from this flour, you will have eaten soba noodles at their absolute best!* (Many shops claim to make handmade, or *te-uchi*, noodles, but the term, as explained in the History section, has become so abused and overused that it has come to be expected by the customer who frequents any nicely decorated soba shop, whether the noodles are handmade or not.)

Few in number, but sharp and biting as the *wasabi* they grate, these masters carry on the traditions of Japanese soba cooking in the spirit of sumo—that is, by a strictly controlled and retained ranking system which, while unspoken, pervades the circles attached to the soba master. There are *yokozuna* (established masters of 20 or more years with considerable fame and following), *ozeki* (10 to 15 years, opening their own shops after years of training), *sekiwake* (3 to 10 years of training), and *maegashira* (trainees). Each of them takes pride in delivering soba according to his own understanding and preferences. Again, as with sumo, many of the masters are born into the "way," and other "newcomers" struggle to get to the top, branching off to spread their master's style of soba-making under their own direction.

While one can learn the stand and machine styles of soba preparation in just a short period of time, the handmade style takes years of training to acquire. What qualifications distinguish good soba shops from the also-rans? Traditionalists and modern soba chefs alike agree that to produce the best soba, the principles encapsulated in the phrase *"Hiki-tate, uchi-tate, yude-tate"* must be upheld. According to this adage the ideal soba is obtained by "using freshly ground flour, making the soba within 2 to 3 hours of serving, and serving it within 1 minute of cooking." (An exception is Soy-Soba Noodles in the Country section.)

Interestingly, nowadays there is a new trend of soba stands proudly displaying signboards claiming to serve soba which satisfies the above three ideal standards. A modern-day version of traditional soba uses soba flour that contains only 30 to 50 percent buckwheat. It is served right upon boiling (*yude-tate*), using machine noodles made fresh that day (*uchi-tate*), from flour ordered from a specialty miller (*hiki-tate*).

They use a lighter-tasting broth, the quality of the accompanying ingredients is high, and they are freshly prepared. As customers line up for this fare day in and day out, one can see that there must be something to this slogan. Less elaborate technique and less refined ingredients notwithstanding, the customers know the taste of good, fresh soba and recognize that at $4.00 a serving these new soba stands are offering a good deal.

Even taking this development into account, however, it's still possible to divide traditional soba-making into two broad categories, *yabu* and *sarashina*, which boast lengthy histories of one and two centuries, respectively.

The *yabu* style features soba which has been made from a rough grinding of the whole buckwheat grain; it is dark in color and sweet in taste. This is the style of soba as it first evolved. A popular and economical fare among laborers of old Tokyo, it originally had an image as a low-class food. The soup which accompanies this soba is made from the "regular" dark soy sauce, which is the basic component in the taste of Tokyo (where lie the roots of the soba business) and which was favored as a good complement to the sweet taste of the dark-colored noodles.

The *sarashina* style features soba made from the center of the grain only. As explained in detail in the Characteristics section, only 18 percent of the buckwheat kernel is made up of this high-grade starch. Correspondingly, the price of this flour is three times that of the more abundant dark-colored flour. This *sarashina* flour is pure white and is either served as a plain white noodle or combined with black sesame seeds, the yellow skin of the *yuzu* citron, and green *shiso* leaves to attain brightly colored Flavored Soba. As the pure-white noodle has an imperceptible taste by itself, the soup which accompanies it is milder than that of the *yabu* style.

Traditional soba shops use only carefully selected ingredients for their stock, paying special attention to making the best taste at a slightly higher cost. In addition, the elegance of the restaurants (interior, utensils, tables, and so on) is also top-class. They use homemade flour (ground fresh daily) or flour of the highest grade costing as much as $120 to $150 per 50-pound bag. The noodles contain 70 to 90 percent buckwheat (30 to 10 percent wheat). The price of a tray of plain soba is about $2.65 to $4.00; and with tempura, $6.65 to $16.65.

To further differentiate these elite 40 to 50 shops would take us beyond the scope of this initial introductory book on soba. Personal preference, background, and experience will lead you to discover your own favorites. In addition, as the apprentices gain confidence and skill, little shops spring up each year like bamboo shoots, making it almost impossible to mention all of the shops worthy of their trade.

Therefore, while not being the last word on the subject, the reviews in this book serve soba that upholds the three *tate*s mentioned above, and will not fail to deliver entrées which will confirm all the claims made for soba in this book.

NOTE: The usage of soba terms for Soba Noodles in a Basket (Mori Soba, or Seiro or Zaru), as well as other dishes, varies slightly from shop to shop. To facilitate your ordering at the soba restaurants included here, the shop's preferred phrasing has been used.

## Fujisei

3–19–13, Nishi Ogi Kita, Suginami-ku, Tokyo
東京都杉並区西荻北3–19–13　☎(03) 395-5453
NEAREST STATION: Nishi-Ogikubo Station, JR Chuo Line
HOURS: 12:00–14:30, 17:30–22:00; Sundays and holidays until 12:00–20:00

Proprietor and master Shigeru Fujimori, 35, has been upholding the *yabu* tradition in fine fashion for over eight years now. After graduating from Aoyama University as a physics major, he discovered the world of soba upon taking a part-time job. The challenge, mystique, and physical nature of the work captured his imagination. He threw away his degree.

After an intensive one-year training with Abe Takeo of Take Yabu, he opened a shop in a quaint residential area, a 30-second walk from Nishi-Ogikubo Station. This is where I worked and trained for three years.

At Fujisei every dish is prepared by the master himself. He serves a noodle that is 90 to 98 percent buckwheat. Using top-of-the-line Kirishita ("Under the Fog") flour, the soba dough requires the addition of only the slightest amount of wheat. He supports the taste with a tangy, well-balanced, strong, but sweet dipping sauce.

Everything is delicious and, equally important, reasonably priced. Especially popular are *Kamo Nanban* (Soba Noodles with Duck, Nov.–Feb, ¥1,500); *Kaki-age Tempura* (¥1,500), a rich sweet and hot Curry Soba (¥900); a light *Natto Soba* (¥800); *Awayuki Soba* (cool noodles topped with whipped egg whites to form a light, fluffy base for an assortment of vegetables, ¥800).

Being a connoisseur of drink as well as food, the master offers a selection of the finest saké. To accompany the saké, Fujisei offers a handful of appetizers including Sliced Sweet Omelette (¥600), Soba Sushi (¥1,500; must be ordered ahead of time), and chicken with onions (¥400; duck in winter). And for dessert there is *Soba Dango* (¥500).

On Saturdays and Sundays, families come to enjoy a hearty meal together at a very reasonable price. If it's crowded, walk around the block and take in the residential college-town atmosphere of Nishi-Ogikubo. The wait is worth it.

**How to get there:** Go out the north exit and walk toward the bus stop in front of the station. Cross the street and turn down the narrow street bracketed by a flower shop and pachinko parlor. Fujisei is on the left, about 15 yards from the corner.

## Honjinbo

Amano Bldg., B1, 1–5–10 Nishi-Shinbashi, Minato-ku, Tokyo
東京都港区西新橋1–5–10　天野ビルB1　☎(03) 508-8166
NEAREST STATION: Uchisaiwai-cho Station, Mita Line; Shinbashi Station, various lines
HOURS: 11:00–21:30; Saturdays and holidays, 11:00–20:00; closed Sundays

After eight successful years in Shinbashi, Honjinbo has moved to a new location in Nishi-Shinbashi. The menu features buckwheat noodles rolled out and cut by hand in the traditional way. If you have always thought that all soba noodles are the same, this shop's menu will be an eye-opener.

Honjinbo's trademark is the daily production of three styles of soba: "plain" (*seiro*), colored (*sarashina*), and thick, dark-brown country-style noodles (*inaka soba*). Honjinbo uses only top-quality buckwheat flours. The plain *seiro* soba, which is light in color, is cut very thin and made from a two-to-eight ratio of wheat to buckwheat. Thinly cut, colored soba combines the pure white inner flour of the buckwheat with fragrant condiments such as yellow *yuzu* citron, green *shiso* leaves, or black sesame seeds. The dark, thickly cut, chewy, "country-style" soba features the outer chocolate-brown, protein-rich, and sweet flour.

Offered in either regular or large (*omori*) sizes, the soba can be ordered individually, two kinds served back to back, or three kinds served one by one. Just as you are finishing your first tray, the second will appear. The third comes just as you are finishing your second, with uncanny timing.

The pleasure of this method of delivery is that although all the noodles have been made from buckwheat, they each have a distinctive taste, texture, and pleasant visual appeal, meaning that you never tire of the always fresh and spicy noodles. The accompanying broth is not as strong as the *yabu* style but nevertheless is stimulating and delicious. In addition, the soup stock for the cool noodles is kept at just the right temperature for the time of year. In summer, you'll never fail to get a refreshingly chilled soup stock. This may sound like a small point, but if you've ever received a lukewarm soup on a hot Tokyo summer day, this is something to be appreciated. The same goes for the temperature of the soba which is dashed over and over again with ice water. The beer and saké are also properly chilled.

Fresh noodles with a serving of tempura, or *Tenseiro*, features two big pieces of crisp and crunchy shrimp, which can be eaten tail and all, accompanied by eggplant and small green pepper. Green tea, which is made individually and served before the meal, is another indication of quality.

With the opening of his new restaurant, Honjinbo's master has assembled a staff of expert chefs to handle the appetizer (*nuki*) cooking, and now offers a variety of dishes, some of which change each week, including Soba Miso, Soba Sushi, and Soba Dumpling (takeout service is also available). This is an experience in fine Japanese dining, featuring the best in buckwheat. Don't miss it.

**How to get there:** Take the A3 exit heading for Toranomon. At the top of the stairs walk toward the crosswalk about 50 yards ahead. Honjinbo is located alongside on the left-hand side, in the basement, and a big house-shaped sign makes its location easily identifiable. From Shinbashi Station, it is a 5- to 7-minute walk down Sotobori-dori heading toward the Hibiya Center. Honjinbo will be on the right-hand side.

## Honke Owari-ya

Nijo Minami Hairu, Kurumaya-cho, Nakagyo-ku, Kyoto
京都市中京区車屋町二条南入ル　☎(075) 231–3446
NEAREST STATION: Oike Station, Karasuma Line
HOURS: 11:00–19:00, closed Wednesdays

This Kyoto soba restaurant is one of the oldest of the old. Established some 520 years ago, it is renowned for maintaining the traditional ways.

The most popular dish is a mini-*Wanko Soba* affair called *Horai Soba* for ¥1,400, which is served with generous amounts of daikon radish (mounded in the center) surrounded by generous portions of shrimp tempura, freshly grated *wasabi* horseradish, bonito flakes, *nori*, and sesame seeds.

**How to get there:** Walk down Karasuma-dori heading toward Nijo-dori. You'll find the shop after 2 to 3 minutes, on your right.

## Honmura-an

2–7–11 Kamiogi, Suginami-ku, Tokyo
東京都杉並区上荻2-7-11　☎(03) 390-0325
NEAREST STATION: Ogikubo Station, JR Chuo Line
HOURS: 11:00–21:00, closed Thursdays

Third-generation master Katsuro began making the homemade style of service seventeen years ago. He is one of the pioneers in home milling and is a highly respected leader of the soba movement in Japan. Using the best domestic harvest of buckwheat, he stone-grinds only what flour is necessary for that day's business (keeping the groats in a cooled warehouse), and proceeds to faithfully follow the famous motto of "freshly ground, freshly made, freshly cooked." Since he uses a rough grind, the noodles are shorter than at other places. This is another demonstration of not bending to customers' whims but rather educating them to a style that is equally meritorious. Once again, order large *omori* portions to begin with.

**How to get there:** Go out the exit nearest Nishi-Ogikubo Station, turn left after passing through the wicket, then right on Kanjo Hachi-go road, the lane that parallels the tracks. You'll see a big picture window–sized billboard indicating the location of the shop, with a map. It takes about 10 minutes on foot. If this proves to be too difficult, take a 3-minute taxi ride.

## Issa-an

1–8–24 Yuki-no-shita, Kamakura, Kanagawa Prefecture
神奈川県鎌倉市雪ノ下1-8-24　☎(0467) 22-3556
NEAREST STATION: Kamakura Station, Yokosuka Line
HOURS: 11:00–19:00; closed some Thursdays

A courtyard with stone lanterns and a fence of bamboo. This shop was a residence in the Taisho period (1912–26). The atmosphere is suitable for an ancient city like Kamakura, where many tourists come to breathe the air of Japan in times gone by. Fortunately, this store doesn't take advantage of its attractive location to skimp on making good-quality soba. Instead, they use the best soba flour available from Hokkaido, as well as from Aomori and Ibaragi prefectures. Flavored Soba is ¥1,000, and plain *sarashina* (white soba) is ¥900. In summer, *Seiro Soba* (¥550) is recommended, and in winter, Wild Duck Soba (*Kamo Nanban Soba*) is recommended. According to season, Yellow Chinese Citron (*Yuzu*) Soba, Black Sesame (*Goma*) Soba, and Green Mugwort (*Yomogi*) Soba are offered and recommended.

**How to get there:** Walk down Sando street toward the Hachiman-gu temple. After 5 to 6 minutes you'll see two large parking lots on the left. The shop is located next door.

## Kuro Mugi

Shin Aoyama Bldg., B1, 1–1–1 Minami Aoyama, Minato-ku, Tokyo
東京都港区南青山1-1-1　新青山ビルB1　☎(03) 475-1850
NEAREST STATION: Aoyama 1-chome Station, Ginza Line
HOURS: 11:30–20:40; Saturdays until 8; holidays, 11:30–21:00; closed Sundays

*Kuro mugi* means black wheat and is one of buckwheat's nicknames. Indeed, this store lives up to its name and serves soba which only a specialist can prepare. Most popular and representative of the dishes served is the entrée *Sanshoku Soba* (green tea, poppy seed, and regular *seiro*, ¥900). They have a beautiful mural of old Edo along one of the walls, and the waitresses are sharp and attentive, so if you work in this area, count yourself lucky and step in for some honest-to-goodness handmade soba.

**How to get there:** Exit Aoyama 1-chome Station and follow the signs to Aoyama Twin Towers.

## Masu-oto

2–25–18 Hirai, Edogawa-ku, Tokyo
東京都江戸川区平井2-25-18　☎(03) 681–5610
NEAREST STATION: Hirai Station, JR Sobu Line
HOURS: 11:00–20:00, closed Thursdays

The master, Hiroyuki Suzuki, 72, has traveled extensively throughout Japan in search of ever-new ways to prepare soba. Over a career spanning sixty years, he has kept detailed notes of his travels and observations about soba. Convinced that the best soba shops never alter their style according to the whims of the customers (who are endlessly saying that the broth should be this way or the noodle that), Suzuki serves modest but graceful portions and in addition has purposely chosen to keep his shop dimly lit and sparsely heated in the winter or too warm in the summer, as if to challenge the customer to enjoy the natural taste of the soba in as natural a setting as possible. In addition, the original colorful artifacts and paintings from the Edo period convincingly evoke the Tokyo of old.

Noodles made from 100-percent buckwheat flour is the master's choice. Using flour from Nagano and Ibaragi (two of the most famous buckwheat regions in Japan), Master Suzuki presents noodles a little thicker than *yabu*, with a nice, sweet taste. Noodles on a Tray (*Mori Soba*) are ¥400; with tempura, ¥1,100.

**How to get there:** Walk straight down the Shopping Mall (*shoten-gai*) for 3 to 5 minutes and you'll find the shop on your right.

## Matsuya

1–13, Kanda Suda-cho, Chiyoda-ku, Tokyo
東京都千代田区神田須田町1-13　☎(03) 251–1556
NEAREST STATION: Awaji-cho Station, Marunouchi Line; Ogawamachi Station, Shinjuku Line
HOURS: 11:00–20:00, closed Sundays and holidays

Located in the heart of Kanda, this shop has been run by the same family for three generations. They use high-quality flour to make the noodles in the traditional way.

The Kodaka family has been traditional soba-makers since 1884. Toshi Kodaka, Matsuya's third-generation proprietor, continues the shop's traditional ways, whose name means Pine House in English. From the monumental bowl for kneading soba dough, carved from horse chestnut wood, dark and glossy with age, to the rustic bamboo and mud-plastered walls, the dark wood ceiling, and the paper-shaded lamps, Matsuya exudes the air of the old Tokyo soba shop and provides a soothing respite from Kanda's busy streets.

At Matsuya, dark buckwheat flour is kneaded with egg yolks to make a rich, brown noodle. Matsuya relies on a five-to-one ratio of buckwheat to wheat flour, with the eggs as an additional binding agent. Matsuya's dipping sauce is a variation on the *yabu* style. The connoisseur could be completely satisfied with the simplest order, Soba Noodles in a Basket—*Hanamaki Soba*. This dish is a stringent test of the quality of soba, since the noodles must stand on their own. Matsuya passes the test, a result of using only the best domestic buckwheat flour and freshly grated *wasabi* horseradish from Izu. *Hanamaki Soba* appears on a small lacquer tray, with a dish of chopped scallions and grated *wasabi*, a pot of dipping sauce, a cup, and chopsticks. Glossy, greenish black flakes of nori seaweed are scattered over the tangle of soba. Other cold soba dishes include *Mori Soba* (without *wasabi* or nori),

*Tararo Soba* (noodles served with the grated yam and *wasabi*), and *Tenzaru* (noodles and hot tempura).

Matsuya's menu of hot soba dishes runs the gamut from *Kitsune* ("Fox") *Soba* to *Okame* ("Rosy-Cheeked") *Soba*. They also offer a very delicious Soba Dumpling (¥750), which has become quite a rarity at soba shops these days.

**How to get there:** Take the A3 exit and walk down Yasukuni street for 2 to 3 minutes heading toward Sudacho street. Matsuya will be on the left-hand side.

## Muromachi Sunaba

4–5–4 Muromachi, Nihonbashi, Chuo-ku, Tokyo
東京都中央区日本橋室町4-5-4  ☎(03) 241-4038
NEAREST STATION: Kanda Station, various lines
HOURS: Weekdays, 11:00–19:30; Sundays and holidays, 11:30–21:00

The original Sunaba is credited as one of the first, if not the first, famous soba shops in Japan. This branch of Sunaba (another family or style in addition to *yabu* and *sarashina*) was established in 1870 and is now in the capable hands of fourth-generation owner Ryoichi Muramatsu, who maintains the shop's policy of putting its all into each job, no matter how small or insignificant it may appear. And the effort shows in the food and the service.

Because of the Great Kanto Earthquake in 1923 and numerous rebuilding in the area, the shop has been moved many times. It settled at the present location fourteen years ago. A well-cared-for garden, easily viewed from the windows of the shop, makes for a relaxed environment right in the middle of the city.

Muromachi Sunaba became the soba-ya that it is today after World War II. Before this it specialized in sweets, and as such it was very similar to the original confection makers credited with giving soba its delicate and refined nature (see History). Today, Muromachi Sunaba is so skillful at protecting the basics of soba cooking that even the critics and reviewers invariably leave satisfied.

Recommendations: Rolled Omelette (*Tamago-yaki*, ¥600) made fresh upon order and served hot is very popular, as are *Zaru* (¥500), *Chikara Soba* (¥850), Chicken Soba (¥850), *Ten-mori* and *Ten-zaru* (¥1,100); the latter two have been served since 1950 in the original style.

**How to get there:** Walk down Chuo-dori toward Mitsukoshi Department Store. Turn right at Muromachi 4-chome Crossing. The shop is 50 yards down on the left.

## Nosatsu-te

2-2-17, Bakuro-cho, Nihonbashi, Chuo-ku, Tokyo
東京都中央区日本橋馬喰町2-2-17  ☎(03) 663-4958
NEAREST STATION: Bakuro-cho Station, JR Sobu Line
HOURS: 11:30–21:00; closed Sundays and holidays

Soba made from 100 percent buckwheat is rolled out in front of the customer in this new-style soba restaurant. A U-shaped counter (seating 15) surrounds master Masao Masuda, and he works his craft right in front of you. The lunchtime menu of *Seiro Soba* (¥1,000), and the large dinner set (¥1,500), draw a full house daily.

The broth is in Tokyo style, deep and rich. Soba Dumpling is available after 1:00 P.M. after the lunch rush is over. The restaurant is decorated with antique short collarless coats on the walls around the counter, and the decor boasts artifacts from the Edo period. The bowls and small saké cups are also carefully matched with the decor.

If you tell the master the number of people and your budget, he will be pleased to make a simple course of *kaiseki*, featuring Soba Sushi and so on.

**How to get there:** Take the Mitsui Bank exit and walk straight for 100 yards to the Sasaki Glass Shop. Turn right and you'll see the shop on the right.

## Okina

2205 Nakamaru, Nagasaka-cho, Kita Koma-gun, Yamanashi Prefecture
山梨県北巨摩郡長坂町中丸2205　☎(0551) 32-5405
NEAREST STATION: Kobuchizawa Station, JR Chuo Hon Line
HOURS: 11:30–15:00

Master Kunihiro Takahashi retired from the life of a company employee after only a short stint due to his uncompromising search for something to satisfy not only the pocketbook but also the soul. He trained with the legendary disseminator of the Issa-an style of soba, Yasuo Katakura, and then opened the Nagasaka Sarashina soba shop in Tokyo in 1974. The purity of his technique and the taste of the soba itself soon made his shop famous throughout Japan. With all this success, he was not satisfied. In 1987 he opened a new shop, away in the beautiful countryside of Nagasaka-cho, near the Shirakaba Museum. Here the only entrées on the menu are fresh (*Seiro*) and country-style (*Inaka Seiro*), both ¥1,000. Appetizers include only saké and freshly ground *wasabi* horseradish!

I visited with Professor Ujihara of Shinshu University, located about an hour's drive away. It was on a snowy Sunday in February, but nevertheless, by one in the afternoon, this "cabin in the woods" soba shop, which seats 40 to 50, was bustling with sight-seeing couples, families, and individuals (coming by taxi) there to taste the real thing. If you are in the area (or just want a destination to shoot for on an outing from Tokyo), this shop is a must.

**How to get there:** From the station it is a 10-minute taxi ride toward Shirakaba Art Museum (Shirakaba Bijitsukan).

## Tagoto Honten

12 Higashi Hairu, Sanjo-dori Teramachi, Nakagyo-ku, Kyoto
京都市中京区三条通寺町東入ル12　☎(075) 221-3030
HOURS: 11:00–21:30; closed Tuesdays

Established in 1925, this Kyoto restaurant keeps its traditional ways of making soba while searching for and developing new variations on the standard 2:8 noodle. Most popular is the *sarashina* noodles (*Misogi Soba*, ¥750), Tempura Soba (¥1,100), and *Tagoto Soba* (hot noodles with nori, and a mound of fresh abalone all garnished with finely chopped scallions).

**How to get there:** Take a bus to the Kawaramachi Sanjo bus stop. Tagoto Honten is located in front of the famous Yata Jizo statue on the right.

## Take Yabu

1144–2 Kashiwa, Kashiwa-shi, Chiba Prefecture
千葉県柏市柏1144-2　☎(0471) 63-9838
NEAREST STATION: Kashiwa Station, JR Joban Line
HOURS: 11:30–20:00; closed Thursdays

After a twenty-year career operating the pacesetting shop of its time right next to the Sogo Department Store Mall in Kashiwa Station, Takeo Abe, 44, decided that he would dispense with the formalities associated with the restaurant business and open up his dream soba shop in the midst of nature, on top of a hill which has the freshest of breezes, 15 minutes from the station. I met Mr. Abe in the spring of 1980.

It was at his first shop in the town that I had my initial encounter with "real soba." I had a cool dish of *Natto Soba*, then Tempura Soba, still sizzling and crackling as it was placed in front of me. Both portions were lean, as if to suggest, "What's your hurry? Why not have another fresh and delicious soba combination?"

The price of his food, even twenty years ago, was always a point of discussion, but he stuck to his guns, saying that only those who really loved soba should come to his shop. He was not making soba just to fill the stomach, but also to elevate the customer's appreciation of the simple things in life: soba was and is his medium and message.

One step into his new restaurant and you know you're in for a different kind of experience. Abe-san's keen natural sense, using the finest lacquer ware to serve his delicate portions of soba, lead many a student of the trade to visit and pick up a few hints.

As Kashiwa is a 30-minute train ride from Ueno, we're talking about a 3-to-4-hour outing, but it's a nice excuse to get out of the big city. The soba is of course of the best, but like the famous *yabu* shops, you need at least 2 or 3 portions to justify your journey. Yet, this is the perfect setting for enjoying soba. Upon visiting this restaurant for the first time back in 1981, I was inspired to delve into the world of soba in earnest. Take Yabu has received wide acclaim as a leader and pacesetter of ever-expanding vision.

Favorite dishes: *Seiro Soba* (¥500), *Kaki-age Tempura Soba* (¥2,000), *Soba Kaiseki* (soba haute cuisine, ¥10,000).

**How to get there:** Turn right out the exit and go down the first set of stairs. You'll find a taxi stand nearby. Ask to be driven to Take Yabu. It's a quick 8 to 10 minutes (¥550).

## Yabu Soba

2–10 Kanda Awaji-cho, Chiyoda-ku, Tokyo
東京都千代田区神田淡路町2-10　☎(03) 251-0287
NEAREST STATION: Awaji-cho Station, Marunouchi Line
HOURS: 11:30–19:00; closed Mondays

This restaurant is famous as the originator and sustainer of the *yabu* style, which goes back over one hundred years. It remains an ever-famous "in" spot of Tokyo.

Two fundamental trademarks found at all three of the *yabu* shops mentioned here are the noodles and the broth. The flour used to make the soba features the protein-rich, sweet-tasting outer part of the buckwheat to obtain a dark-brown, firm, and chewy country-style soba. This is combined with a strong blend of bonito stock, soy sauce, and *mirin*, sugar-blended and balanced in the traditional *yabu* way. This is the strong, stimulating dipping sauce that the common laborers building the capital city of Tokyo during the Edo period (1600–1868) were so fond of.

The portions are modest, so you will probably have to order extra-large portions (*omori*) or even three trays of cooled soba (*seiro*) to be satisfied. (One tray costing ¥400 is referred to as *mori*, or you can pay ¥500 with nori, which is referred to as *Hanamaki Soba*). The *kaki-age* style of tempura (¥1,100), and in winter Wild Duck Soba (*Kamo-nanban Soba*, ¥1,100), are also *yabu* standards whose popularity never fades, and even with the slim portions, customers always come back again and again. Maybe all Westerners should order large portions and consider it done with. Also recommended is Soba Sushi (¥550). If you go at peak hours, be prepared for a full house.

**How to get there:** Heading for Yushima-dori, walk 2 to 3 minutes down Sotobori-dori. You'll find the shop on Sotobori-dori just before the Kanda Post Office.

# ADDITIONAL SHOPS

## Ichiei

3–9–5 Higashi Ikebukuro, Toshima-ku, Tokyo
東京都豊島区東池袋3–9–5　☎(03) 987–7051
NEAREST STATION: Ikebukuro, various lines
HOURS: 11:30–20:30; closed Sundays and holidays

**How to get there:** Exit the Seibu Department Store side of the station. Walk down Meiji-dori toward Kami Ikebukuro until you reach the five-cornered crossing (Tokyo Gas will be on the left). Pass under the highway and take the second street on your right. The shop is on the second block on the right.

## Nanaki

1–13–2 Ebisu Nishi, Shibuya-ku, Tokyo
東京都渋谷区恵比寿西1–13–2　☎(03) 496–2878
NEAREST STATION: Ebisu Station, JR Yamanote Line or Hibiya Line
HOURS: 11:30–21:30

**How to get there:** Go out the main exit of Ebisu Station (on the Yamanote Line). Make a sharp right, cross the street, turn left and then right at Wendys. The shop is across the street at the end of the block.

## Shinano

2–10 Kagurazaka, Shinjuku-ku, Tokyo
東京都新宿区神楽坂2–10　☎(03) 269–1411
NEAREST STATION: Iidabashi Station, JR Chuo Line
HOURS: 11:00–20:30; closed Sundays and holidays

**How to get there:** Hand in your ticket at the exit nearest the Ichigaya side of the station and walk 5 minutes down the Kagurazaka Shopping Mall (*shoten-gai*). Turn right at Kinoben Confectionery. The shop is on your left.

## Shinshu Sarashina

3–11–4 Moto Azabu, Minato-ku, Tokyo
東京都港区元麻布3–11–4　☎(03) 403–3401
NEAREST STATION: Roppongi, Hibiya Line
HOURS: 11:30–20:30; closed Wednesdays

**How to get there:** Turn down the narrow street that runs alongside the Almond Coffee Shop toward the Ni-no-hashi Crossing. The shop is a 15-minute walk, on the right one block before the crossing.

## Sunaba

3–11–13 Toranomon, Minato-ku, Tokyo
東京都港区虎ノ門3–11–13　☎(03) 431–1220
NEAREST STATION: Kamiya-cho, Hibiya Line
HOURS: 11:00–19:30; Saturdays until 14:00; closed Sundays

**How to get there:** Exit the stairwell leading to Fuji Bank (toward Toranomon). Walk down Sakurada-dori toward Toranomon. The shop is 5 minutes from the exit on the right side.

# Oriental, Natural, and Specialty Food Stores in the United States and Canada

## United States

### ALABAMA

Asian Super Market
1407–A Montgomery Hwy
Birmingham 35216

Ebino Oriental Store
323 Air Base Blvd
Montgomery 36108

Japanese Grocery
2007 University Dr
Huntsville 35210

### ARIZONA

Gentle Strength Co-op
234 W. University
Tempe 85281

Reay's Ranch Market
3360 E. Speedway
Tucson 85716

### CALIFORNIA
North

ABC Fish & Ort'l Fd
1911 Portrero Way
Sacramento 95822

Asahi-ya
229 East Alpine Ave
Stockton 95009

Asia Food Market
2000 Judah St
San Francisco 94122

Asian Products
St Francis Sq, #39
Daly City 94015

Berkeley Bowl
27777 Shattuk Ave
Berkeley 94705

Bread of Life
1690 S. Bascom Ave
Campbell 95008

Brother's Oriental Mkt
37365 Fremont Blvd
Fremont 94536

Castro City Grocery
405 Rengstorff Ave
Mountain View 94040

Community Foods
2724 Soquel
Santa Cruz 95062

Community Market
1215 Morgan St
Santa Rosa 95401

Country Sun
440 California Ave
Palo Alto 94306

Diablo Oriental Food
2590 N. Main St
Walnut Creek 94596

Dobashi
240 E. Jackson St
San Jose 95112

Easy Food
299 Castro St
Mountain View 94040

Erewhon Natural Fd
8001 Beverly Blvd
Los Angeles 90048

Eugene Food
335–14th St
Oakland 94612

First Food Market
4454 California St
San Francisco 94118

Food Center Market
1912 Fruitridge
Sacramento 95822

Happy Produce
1240 Solano Ave
Albany 94706

International Market
2019 Fillmore St
San Francisco 94115

Jack's Food Center
519 E. Charter Way
Stockton 95206

Keiko Oriental
3417 Chestnut Ave
Concord 94519

Kiely Market
1074 Kiely Blvd
Santa Clara 95051

Living Foods
222 Greenfield
San Anselmo 94960

Living Foods #3
1581 University
Berkeley 94703

Marina Oriental Food
215 Reservation Rd
Marina 93933

Maruwa Food
1737 Post St
San Francisco 94115

Maruwa Morio of America
1092 E. El Camino Real
Sunnyvale 94087

Metro Food
641 Broadway
San Francisco 94133

Miko's Japanese Fd
524 Tuolumne
Vallejo 94590

Musashi Oriental Fd
962 W. El Camino Real
Sunnyvale 94087

Nakagawa
306 C St
Marysville 95901

Nishioka Fish Market
665 N. Sixth St
San Jose 95112

Nomura Market
29583 Mission Blvd
Hayward 94544

Nori's
1119 West Texas
Fairfield 94533

Oakland Market
378 8th St
Oakland 94607

Organic Grocery
2481 Guerneville Rd
Santa Rosa 95401

Oriental Food Fair
10368 San Pablo Ave
El Cerrito 94530

Oriental Food Store
9189 Kiefer Blvd
Sacramento 95826

Oriental Market
413–B San Antonio Rd
Mountain View 94040

Oriental Store
3443 El Camino Real
Santa Clara 95051

Orient Grocery
337 8th St
Oakland 94612

Otto's Japan Food
5770 Freport Blvd
Sacramento 95822

Pacific Food Center
1924 4th St
San Rafael 94901

Pacific Grocery
1125 Stockton St
San Francisco 94133

Parade Food Store
145 Jackson St
Hayward 94544

Rainbow Grocery
1899 Mission St
San Francisco 94103

Real Foods #2
3939 24th St
San Francisco 94114

Real Foods #3
2140 Polk St
San Francisco 94109

Sacramento Natural Fd
2996 Freeport Blvd
Sacrament 95816

Safeway Store #592
7th & Cabrillo St
San Francisco 94118

Safeway Store #785
850 La Playa
San Francisco 94121

K Sakai (Uoki)
1656 Post St
San Francisco 94115

Santos Market
245 E. Taylor St
San Jose 95112

Save Mart #3
6045 N. El Dorado St
Stockton 95207

Star Fish Market
320 S. El Dorado St
Stockton 95203

Sunrise Grocery
400 Pearl St
Monterey 93940

Super Save Market
39 W. Chatterway
Stockton 95206

Suruki
140 Boothbay
Foster City 94404

Takahashi
221 S. Claremont St
San Mateo 94401

Tim's Market
310 7th St
Oakland 94607

Vickie's Oriental Food
157-8 Parker St
Vacaville 95688

Waki's Fish Market
1335 S. Lincoln St
Stockton 95206

South

A. A. Supermarket
3030 W. Sepulveda Blvd
Torrance 90505

Albertson's
Head Office:
200 North Puente
Brea, CA. 92621
(714) 529-9911

Long Beach (#1905),
Los Angeles (3443 S.

Sepulveda Blvd, #668),
Montebello (#603),
Monterey Park (#626)

Aloha Grocery
4515 Centinella Ave
Los Angeles 90066

Aloha Market
900 West Main St
Santa Maria 93454

Alpha Beta
Head Office:
777 South Harbor Blvd
La Habra, CA. 90631
(714) 738-2000

Buena Park, Carson,
Cerritos, Costa Mesa,
Culver City, Glendale,
Hollywood,
Lakewood, La Palma,
Long Beach, Los
Angeles (2740 W.
Olympic Blvd, 420 W.
Olympic Blvd),
Monterey Park,
Rowland Heights,
Santa Ana

Asahi Market
660 Oxnard Blvd
Oxnard 93030

Best Foods Markets
3030 Sepulveda Blvd
Torrance 90505

Boy's Market
Head Office:
5531 Monte Vista St
Los Angeles, CA
(213) 258-8080

Carson (#48), Gardena
(#13), Lawndale (#56),
Los Angeles (3670
Crenshaw Blvd, #54;
1748 W. Jefferson
Blvd, #15; 1091 S.
Hoover St, #28; 833 S.
Western Ave, #52),
Torrance (#23)

Cathay Supermarket
3969 Beverly Blvd
Los Angeles 90004

Cathay Supermarket
709 N. Hill St
Los Angeles 90012

Community Market
745 First St
Encinitas 92024

Daimaru Market
11360 Beach Blvd
Stanton 90680

Diho Market #1
720 S. Atlantic Blvd
Monterey Park 91754

Diho Market #2
1120 S. Bristol St
Santa Ana 92704

Diho Market #3
15333 Gale Ave
City of Industry 91744

Diho Market #6
11700 E. 183rd St
Artesia 90701

Do Re Mi Grocery Mkt
9520 Garden Grove
Garden Grove 92644

Do Re Mi Grocery Mkt
4301 W. 3rd St
Los Angeles 90020

Do Re Mi Grocery Mkt
1165 N. Euclid
Anaheim 92801

East-West Food Center
3300 W. 8th St
Los Angeles 90005

Ebisu Market
18940 Brookhurst St
Fountain Valley 92708

Eiko Shoten
6082 University Ave
San Diego 92115

Enbun
124 Japanese Village
Los Angeles 90012

Food Basket
Chula Vista (#206),
National City (#212),
Oceanside (#231), San
Diego (6061 El Cajon
Blvd, #201; 4516
Mission Blvd, #202;
6501 University Ave,
#204), Vista (#232)

Foods For Life
504 E. Broadway
Glendale 91205

Fujiya Market
601 N. Virgil Ave
Los Angeles 90004

Fukuda's
242 W. Mission Ave
Escondido 92025

Gooch's
12905 Riverside Dr
Sherman Oaks 91403

Gooch's
9530 Reseda Blvd
Northridge 91354

Gooch's
526 Pier Ave
Hermosa Beach 90254

Green Tree Grocers
3560 Mt Acadia Blvd
San Diego 92112

Hughes Markets
Head Office:
2716 San Fernando Rd
Los Angeles, CA 90065
(213) 227-8211

Beverly Hills (#24),
Burbank (1100 N. San
Fernando Rd, #12;
1028 S. San Fernando
Rd, #25), Canoga Park
(#21), Chatsworth
(#10), Fountain Valley
(#33), Granada Hills
(#4), Hollywood (#26),
Los Angeles (11361
National Blvd, #9),
Mission Hills (#13),
Monterey Park (#15),
Newberry Park (#29),
Newport Beach (3433
Via Lido Dr, #19),
North Hollywood
(#11), Oxnard (#14),
Pacific Palisades (#5),
Palos Verdes (#20),
Pasadena (#30),
Sherman Oaks (#7),
Thousand Oaks,
Torrance (#28),
Valencia (#27)

Hughes-El Rancho Mkt
Huntington Beach
(#46), Irvine (#48),
Laguna Beach (#49),
Newport Beach (2555
E. Bluff Dr, #44)

Jay's Market
4000 W. Pico Blvd
Los Angeles 90019

Kawa Market #2
5410 Magnolia Ave
Riverside 92506

Kawa Market #3
6570 Van Nuys Blvd
Van Nuys 91401

Lucky Stores
Head Office:
6565 Knott Ave
Buena Park, CA 90620
(714) 739-2200

Carson (#435),

Huntington Beach
(#483), Long Beach
(#454), Los Angeles
(133 W. Ave 45, #463),
Montebello (#457),
Redondo Beach (#638),
Riverside (#672), San
Pedro (#623), Torrance
(#655), W. Los Angeles
(3456 Sepulveda Blvd,
#426), Westminster
(#496)

Marukai
15725 S. Vermont Ave
Gardena 90247

Modern Food Market
318 East 2nd St
Los Angeles 90012

Mother's Market
225 E. 17th St
Costa Mesa 92627

Motoyama Market
16135 S. Western Ave
Gardena 90247

New Meiji Market
1620 W. Redondo Beach
Gardena 90247

Nijiya
3860 Convoy St #121
San Diego 92111

Olympic Market
3122 W. Olympic Blvd
Los Angeles 90006

Olympic Market #2
100 S. Western Ave
Los Angeles 90004

Omori's
2700 N. Santa Fe
Vista 92083

Quinn's Market
226 N. Larchmont Blvd
Los Angeles 90004

Quinn's Market
4140 Pacific Coast Hwy
Torrance 90505

Quinn's Market
11251 National Blvd
W. Los Angeles 90064

Quinn's Natural Fd Ctr
18425 Burbank Blvd
Tarzana 91356

Ralph's Groc
Head Office:
1100 W. Artesia Blvd
Compton, CA 96220

(213) 637-1101
Anaheim (88 E.
Orangethorpe, 121 N.
Beach Blvd), Buena
Park, Canoga Park,
Gardena, Hollywood,
Inglewood, Long
Beach, Los Angeles
(7257 Sunset Blvd;
1010 S. Western; 4641-
5 Santa Monica; 3456
W. Third St; 12057
Wilshire Blvd; 2750 E.
First St), Lynwood,
Northridge, Norwalk,
Pomona, Redondo
Beach, Santa Ana,
Torrance, West
Covina

Safe & Save Market
2040 Sawtelle Blvd
West Los Angeles
90025

Safeway
Head Office:
12200 Bellflower Blvd
Downey, CA 90241
(213) 923-7531
Delano (#319),
Glendale (#201), Los
Angeles (2511 Daly St,
#119; 727 N. Vine St,
#128; 4030 Centinela
Ave, #1032; 11674
Santa Monica Blvd,
#133), Montebello
(#1030), Rolling Hills
(#181), San Diego
(4145 30th St, #1441;
6935 Linda Vista Rd,
#1471), Santa Ana
(#408), South
Pasadena (#555),
Sunnymead (#286),
West Hollywood
(#129)

Sakae Oriental Groc
4227 Convoy St
San Diego 92111

Senri Market
111 N. Lincoln Ave
Monterey Park 91754

Valley Oriental Mkt
15331 Parthenia St
Sepulveda 91343

Van Nuys Ort'l Mkt
13723 Oxnard St
Van Nuys 91401

Von's Groc
Head Office:
10150 Lower Azusa Rd

El Monte, CA 91731
(818) 579-1400
Gardena (#14), Harbor
City (#102),
Huntington Beach
(#90), Los Angeles
(3334 W. 8th St, #8;
1020 S. Crenshaw
Blvd, #10; 3644 W.
Santa Barbara Ave,
#15; 3118 S. Sepulveda
Blvd, #77; 124 N.
Western Ave, #87;
9860 W. National
Blvd, #100), Marina
Del Rey (#105),
Montecito (#101),
Pasadena (#152), Santa
Barbara (#109), Santa
Monica (#2), San
Pedro (#85), South
Pasadena (#75)

Western Market
230 S. Western Ave
Los Angeles 90004

Williams Bros #15
1650 Grand Ave
Arroyo Grande 93420

Yaohan
2121 W. 182nd St
Torrance 90504

Yaohan
333 S. Alameda St
Los Angeles 90013

COLORADO

Alfalfa #2
5910 S. Univercity
Littleton 80121

Ann's Oriental Groc
315 Arvada St
Colorado Springs 80906

Havana Oriental Mkt
812 S. Havana St
Aurora 80012

Rainbow Grocery
2260 E. Colfax
Denver 80206

CONNECTICUT

Cheese & Stuff
P.O. Box 87
Hartford 06141

East/West Trading
68 Howe St
New Haven 00511

DELAWARE

Oriental Grocery
1705 Concord Pike
Wilmington 19803

FLORIDA

Chamberlin's Natural Fd
420 N. Orlando Ave
Winter Park 32789

Far Eastern Bazaar
73 Sailfish Dr
Atlantic Beach 32233

Japanese Fish Market
1521 E. Commercial
Ft Lauderdale 33308

Japanese Market
1412 N.E. 79th St
North Bay 33141

Misak's Oriental Store
129 New Warrington Rd
N. Pensacola 32406

Nature Works
461 N. Harbor City
Melbourne 32935

Natures Food Patch
1408 Cleveland
Clearwater 34615

Oak Feed Store
3030 Grand Ave
Coconut Grove 33133

Oriental Imports
2001 E. Colonial Dr
Orlando 32803

Pineapples
530 Arthur Godfrey Rd
Miami Beach 33140

Second Nature
521 N.W. 13th St
Gainesville 32601

Stubb's Oriental Food
807 East Ave
Panama City 32401

Tokyo Food Market
1703 N. Wickham Rd
Melbourne 32935

Tomiko's Ort'l Store
441 Bryn Athyn Blvd
Mary Esther 32569

Unicorn Village
16454 N.E. 6th Ave
Miami 33162

Wholly Harvest

4616 S. Dixie Hwy
West Palm Beach 33405

Yates Bros Produce
4601 Haines Rd
St Petersburg 33710

GEORGIA

Atlanta Oriental Fd
3114 Oakcliff Ind St
Doraville 30340

First Oriental Market
2595 N. Decatur Rd
Decatur 30033

Nippan Daido
2390 Carroll Ave
Chamblee 30341

Satsuma–ya
1849 Cobb Pkwy
Marietta 30062

Sevananda Natural Fd
1111 Enclid Ave
Atlanta 30307

Shop & Go Oriental
2595 Laurenceville Hwy
Decatur 30033

United Food
765–B Clay St
Marietta 30060

World Super Market
2579 N. Decatur Rd
Decatur 30033

IDAHO

Albertson's
Box 20
Boise 83707

Boise Consumer Co-op
1674 Hill Rd
Boise 83702

ILLINOIS

J–R Ort'l Food Mart
1109 N. Western Ave
Chicago

Kishu-ya
6036 W. Dempster St
Morton Grove

New City Market
1810 N. Halsted
Chicago 60614

Oriental Treasure Ctr
675 N. Cass Ave
Westmont

Sherwyn's Health Fd
645 W. Diversey
Chicago 60614

Shinanoya Market
940 W. Algonquin Rd
Arlington Hts

Sunset Foods
1812 Green Bay Rd
Highland Park

Super-Saver Ort'l Fd
7109 North Western
Chicago

Co-op Supermarket
1526 East 55th St
Chicago 60615

Fuji Enterprises
4138 Church St
Skokie 60076

Golf Oriental Food
9142 Golf Rd
Des Plaines 60016

Kampai
2330 S. Elmhurst Rd
Mt Prospect 60056

Koyama
2482 East Oakton Rd
Arlington 60005

Momi Food
4971 N. Elston Ave
Chicago 60630

Sakura of Tokyo
1163 Ogden Ave
Naperville 60540

Yamasho
354 Lively Blvd
Elk Grove Village 60007

INDIANA

Bloomingfoods
19 East Kirkwood
Bloomington 47401

Good Earth Foods
6350 W. Guilford Ave
Indianapolis 46220

IOWA

East-West Oriental Fd
624 S. Gilbart St
Iowa City

Good Earth Nutrition
1415 South Federal
Mason City

Oriental Food Store
401 Brady St
Davenport

KANSAS

Asian Supermarket
9538 Nall-Nall Hills
Overland Park

Beak Oriental Foods
1032 Minnesota Ave
Kansas City

Manhattan Food
714 N. 3rd St
Manhattan

LOUISIANA

Au Natural Food
5517 Magazine St
New Orleans 70115

Eve's Market
7700 Cohn St
New Orleans 70118

Oriental Food
3324 Transcontinental
Metairie 70003

Oriental Merutan
2636 Edden Borne
Metairie 70002

Oriental Supermarket
3562 S. Carollton Ave
New Orleans 70118

MARYLAND

Arirang House
7918 Georgia Ave
Silver Spring 20910

Asia House
1576 Annapolis Rd
Odenton 21113

Diskor
8476 Piney Branch Rd
Silver Spring 20903

Far East House
33 W. North Ave
Baltimore 21201

Fumi Oriental Mart
2102 Veirs Mill Rd
Rockville 20852

Gourmet's Delight
8775 N. Cloudleap Ct
Columbia 21045

Holiday Mart
Rt 04 Box 12
Smithsburg 21783

The Oriental House
409 E. 32nd St
Baltimore 21218

Village Market
7006 Reisterstown Rd
Owings Mills 21215

MASSACHUSETTS

Bread & Circus
115 Prospect St
Cambridge 02139

Bread & Circus
392 Harvard St
Brookline 02146

Bread & Circus
Rte 9 Russell St
Hadley 01035

Bread & Circus
155 No Beacon St
Brighton 02135

Bread & Circus
278 Washington St
Wellesley Hills 02181

Mirim Trading
152 Harvard Ave
Allston 02134

Yoshinoya
36 Prospect St
Cambridge 02139

MICHIGAN

Arbor Farms
2215 W. Stadium
Ann Arbor 48103

Asia Mart Ort'l Groc
2903 E. Big Beaver
Troy 48083

Asia Trading
734 S. Washington
Royal Oak 48067

Fourth Ave Food Co-op
212 N. Fouth Ave
Ann Arbor 48104

Good Food
33521 West B Mile Rd
Livonia 46152

Grande Gourmet
434 Frandor Ave
Lansing 48912

International Gourmet
18609 Eureka Rd
Southgate 48195

Oryana Food Co-op
601 Randolph St
Traverse City 49684

Packard Co-op
722 Packard
Ann Arbor 48104

People's Food Co-op
212 N. Fourth Ave
Ann Arbor 48104

Zerbo's Health Foods
34164 Plymouth Rd
Livonia 48150

MINNESOTA
Eastern Mkt
8007 Allen
Allen Park 48101

Far East Food Fair
15550 King
Riverview 48192

Fuji-ya
420 S. 1st St
Minneapolis

Market Foods Int'l
730 Kasota Circle
Minneapolis

Midwestern Asian Food
633 W. Minnehaha
St Paul

Oriental Plaza
607 Cedar Ave
Minneapolis

United Noodle
2015 E. 24th St
Minneapolis 55404

MISSOURI
Far Eastern Food Ctr
7611 Wornall Rd
Kansas City

NEBRASKA
Asian Market
808 Fort Crook Rd
S. Bellevue

Oriental Market
12654 Q St
Omaha

NEVADA
Oriental Food
953 E. Sahara E-31
Las Vegas 89104

Tokyo
3344 Kietzke Lane
Reno 89502

NEW JERSEY
Aki Oriental Food
1635 Lemoine Ave
Fort Lee 07024

Asian Food Market
217 Summit Ave
Jersey City 07306

Daido International
1385 16th St Fort Lee
07024

The Health Shoppe
66 Morris St
Morristown 07960

Teri Lee
225 Maywood Ave
Maywood 07607

The Third Day
220 Park Ave
East Rutherford 07073

NEW MEXICO
Alameda Market
627 W. Alemada
Santa Fe 87501

Fremont Fine Foods
556 Coronado Ctr N.E.
Albuquerque 87110

La Montineta Co-op
3500 Central S.E.
Albuquerque 87106

Market Place
808 Early St
Santa Fe 87501

Yonemoto Bros
8725 4th St N.W.
Albuquerque 87114

NEW YORK
Aiya Mart
41-85 Bowne St
Flushing 11354

Commodities
117 Hudson St
New York 10013

Down to Earth
33 S. Seventh Ave
New York 10011

Five Continental Foods
80-19 Broadway El
Elmhurst 11373

Global Food
80-06 Roosevelt Ave
Jackson Heights 11372

Harumi
318-320 W. 231 St
Bronx 10463

Health Hut
18 W. Circle Dr
Vallery Stream 11581

Health Nut
2611 Broadway
New York 10025

Health Nuts
1208 2nd Ave & 63rd
New York 10021

Health Nuts
2141 Broadway
New York 10023

Integral Yoga
227 W. 13th
New York 10011

Katagiri
224 East 59th St
New York 10022

Main St Foods
41-54 Main St
Flushing 11355

Meidiya
18 N. Central Park Ave
Hartsdale 10530

Meiji-ya
2642 Central Ave
Yonkers 10710

Nippan Daido
522 Mamaroneck Ave
White Plains 10605

Nippon Do
82-69 Parsons Blvd
Jamaica 11432

Oriental Groc & Prod
2460 Nesconset Hwy
Stonybrook 11790

Prana
125 1st Ave
New York 10003

Quantun Leap
65-62 Fresh Meadows
Fresh Meadow 11365

Rising Tide
42 Forest Ave
Glen Cove 11542

Shinsendo

1285 East Boston Post
Mamaroneck 10543

Sunnyside Ort'l Fd
47-01 Queens Blvd
Sunnyside 11104

Tomon
5678 Mosholu Ave
Bronx 10471

Whole Foods
117 Prince St
New York 10012

NORTH CAROLINA
McCoy's Japanese Store
1616 Piney Green Rd
Jacksonville 28540

Miwa Oriental Foods
Rt Box 178A
Havelock 28532

Wellspring Grocery
737 Ninth St
Durham 27705

NORTH DAKOTA
Japan Food Products
2158-B Dogwood Dr
Grand Forks AFB

OHIO
Bexley Natural Fd
508 N. Cassidy
Bexley 43209

Cincinnati Natural Fd
7754 Camanga Rd
Cincinnati 45243

Cincinnati Fd Empor.
9268 Colerain Ave
Cincinnati 45239

Dayton Oriental Foods
812 Xenia Ave
Dayton 45410

New World Food Shop
347 Ludlow Ave
Cincinnati 45232

Omura Japanese Food
3811 Payne Ave
Cleveland 44114

Oriental Food
4738 E. Main St
Columbus 43213

Oriental Food & Gifts
500 W. Main St
Fairborn 45324

Soya Food Products
2356 Wyoming Ave
Cincinnati 45214

Tokyo Oriental Foods
11167 Main St
Sharonville 45241

Weber Health Foods
18400 Euclid Ave
Cleveland 44112

OKLAHOMA

Japan Imported Foods
808 N.W. 6th St
Oklahoma City 73106

OREGON

Albertsons #544
12060 S.W. Main
Tigard 97223

Anzen Importers
736 N.E. Union Ave
Portland 97232

Fred Meyers
100 N.W. 20th Pl
Portland 97209

Fred Meyers
777 Kings Blvd
Corvallis 97330

Nature's Fresh N.W.
5909 S.W. Corbett
Portland 97201

Nature's Fresh N.W.
3449 N.E. 24th Ave
Portland 97201

PENNSYLVANIA

Asia Products
226 N. 10th St
Philadelphia 19107

Essene
320 S. South St
Philadelphia 39142

Euro-Asian Imports
5221 E. Simpson Ferry
Mechanicsburg 17055

Imported Food Bazaar
2000 Market St
Camp Hill 17011

Oriental Food Mart
909 Race St
Philadelphia 19107

Oriental Food Store
502 Tilghman St
Allentown 18102

Sundance Natural Food
748 E. 24th St
Eugene 97405

The Oriental
804 South 12th St
Philadelphia 19147

RHODE ISLAND

East Sea Oriental Mkt
90–92 Warren Ave
E. Providence 02914

Persimmon Ort'l Mkt
University Hghts Shop Ctr
Providence 02906

SOUTH CAROLINA

Chieko Hardy
226 Jamaica St
Columbia 29206

Sachi's Oriental Groc
54 Brabham Dr
Dalzell 29040

SOUTH DAKOTA

Kitty's Oriental Food
P.O. Box 347
Box Elder 57719

TENNESSEE

Cherry Blossom
1823 Memorial Blvd
Murefreesboro 37130

Kikuya
400 21st Ave St
Nashville 37203

Sun Oriental Foods
697 Mendenhall St
Memphis 38122

TEXAS

Asiatic Imports
821 Chartres
Houston 77003

Diho Supermarket
9280 Bellaire Blvd
Houston 77036

D.S. Market
10560 Walnut St
Dallas 75243

Dynasty Supermarket
9600 Bellaire Blvd
Houston 77036

Eastern Foods
8626–1/2 Long Point
Houston 77055

Eastern Steamer Supply
3143 Produce Row
Houston 77023

Edoya Oriental
223 Farmer Branch
Dallas 75234

First Oriental Market
904 St Emanuel
Houston 77003

Irving Soul Market
922 E. 6th St
Irving, Texas 75060

Kazy's Food Mart
8989 Forest Lane #106
Dallas 75243

Kobawoo Oriental
5732 Cedar Springs
Dallas 75235

Ko-Ko's Oriental Food
8001 Bangor Dr
Fort Worth 76116

New World Food
176 Farmer Branch
Dallas 75234

Nippon Daido Int'l
11138 Westheimer
Houston 77042

Sachiko Oriental
2504 Loop 410 S.W.
San Antonio 78227

Squash Blossom Mrkt
1720 Popular Ave
Menphis 33104

Sunshine Grocery
1912 Broadway
Nashville 33303

Tachibana
4886 Hercules Ave
El Paso 79904

Terrace Oriental Mrkt
400 N. Greenville
Richardson 75081

Tokyo Mart
819 W. Hildebrand
San Antonio 78212

Whole Foods Market
914 W. Lamar
Austin 78703

Whole Foods Market
9070 Research #201
Austin 78758

Whole Foods Market

4006 S. Lamar
Austin 76704

Whole Foods Market
2218 Greenville Ave
Dallas 75206

Whole Foods Market
2900 S. Shepberd
Houston 77098

World Food
1759 W. 34th St
Houston 77018

UTAH

Oriental Mini-Mart
1786 West 5300 South
Roy 84067

Sage Farm Market
1515 South Main
Salt Lake City 84115

VIRGINIA

China Grocery
3509 S. Jefferson St
Baileys Crossroad 22041

Oriental House
7816 Richmond Hwy
Alexandria 22306

Super Asian Market
2719 Wilson Blvd
Arlington 22201

Tokyo Market
5312 Virginia Beach Blvd
Virginia Beach 23462

Top Meat Market
1537 North Quaker
Alexandria 22302

WASHINGTON

Albertsons
157 N Town Shop Ctr
Spokane 99207

Public Warehouse Mart
West 3330 Central Ave
Spokane 99208

Puget Community Co-op
6504 20th N.E.
Seattle 98115

Puget Consumers Co-op
5028 Roosevelt Hwy
Seattle 98105

Puget Consumers Co-op
10710 N.E. 68th
Kirkland 98033

Puget Consumers Co-op
6522 Freemont
Seattle 98103

Puget Consumers Co-op
50401 Wilson Aves S
Seward Park 98118

QFC #807
4547 Univ Village Plz
Seattle 98105

R & R Food Center
East 628th–9th Ave
Spokane 99204

Safeway Stores, #221
West 2101 Wellsley
Spokane 99205

Safeway #435
9250 Rainier Ave S
Seattle 98118

Safeway #472
3903 Factoria Mall
Bellevue 98006

Safeway #496
15000 24th Ave N.E.
Redmond 98052

Umajimaya
519 6th Ave S
Seattle 98104

Umajimaya-Bellevue
15555 N.E. 24th
Bellevue 98007

Umajima-Southcenter
Southcenter Mall
Tukwila 98188

Villa Thriftco
10110 Gravelly Lake
Tacoma 98499

WASHINGTON, D.C.

Da Hua Food
617 I St N.W.
20001

Hugos
3813–17 Livingston N.W.
20015

House of Hanna
7838 Eastern Ave
20012

Mikado
4709 Wisconsin N.W.
20016

Yes Natural Gourmet
1015 Wisconsin N.W.
20007

WISCONSIN

Intl House of Foods
440 W. Gorham St
Madison 53704

K. P. Oriental Groc
321 N. 27th St
Milwaukee 53208

Peace Oriental Foods
4250 W. Fond du Lac
Milwaukee 53216

## Canada

ALBERTA

Allwest Supermarket
5720 Silverspring N.W.
Calgary

Calgary Co-op #9
2520 52nd St N.E.
Calgary

Canada Safeway
11715 108th Ave N.W.
Edmonton

Edmonton Co-op #3
17010 90th Ave N.W.
Edmonton

IGA
5105 17th Ave S.E.
Calgary

BRITISH COLUMBIA

Canada Safeway #18
1300 Lonsdale
North Vancouver

IGA Stores
4469 Kingsway
Burnaby

Mihamaya
392 Powell St
Vancouver

Shimizu Shoten
349 East Hasting St
Vancouver

Strong's Supermarket
4326 Dunbar St
Vancouver

Super Valu #130
4567 Lougheed Hwy
Burnaby

Super Valu #140
1020 Park Royal
West Vancouver

Super Valu #141
555 6th St
New Westminster

NOVA SCOTIA

Rose Marie Ort'l Gmt
1532 Queen St
Halifax

Wok's Ort'l Gourmet
131 Wyse Rd
Dartmouth

ONTARIO

Fairway Trading
9 Byward Market
Ottawa

Furuya Trading
460 Dundas St West
Toronto

Imported Oriental Fd
270 N. Cumberland St
Thunder Bay

Kealson's
2501 Eglinton Ave East
Scarborough

King Wah Variety
89 York St
London

Nakanishi Japan Food
465 Somerset St West
Ottawa

Pan Asia Food
257 Dundas St East
Mississauga

Sandown Market
221 Kennedy Rd
Scarborough

Sandown Market
826 Brown's Line
Toronto

University Variety
150 University Ave
Waterloo

Yanagawa Japanese Fd
584 Upper James St
Hamilton

QUEBEC

Leong Jung
999 Rue Clark
Montreal

Miyamoto Foods
382 Victoria Ave
Montreal (Westmount)

# Bibliography

Aihara, Cornellia. *The Do of Cooking.* Vol. 1. Oroville, Calif.: G.O.M.F. Publishing, 1972.

Aihara, Herman. *Basic Macrobiotics.* Tokyo: Japan Publications, 1985.

Aihara, Herman. *Macrobiotics: A Key to Happiness.* Oroville, Calif.: G.O.M.F. Publishing, 1977.

Campbell, C. G. "Buckwheat Fagopyrum (Polygonaceae)." In *Evolution of Crop Plants.* Ed. N. W. Simmonds. London and New York: Longman, 1976.

Coe, Maynard R. "Buckwheat Milling and Its By-Products." U. S. Department of Agriculture Circular no. 190. Washington: December 1931.

De Candolle, Alphonse. *The Origin of Cultivated Plants.* 1881. Reprinted as part of the International Scientific Series. New York: D. Appleton and Company, 1908.

De Jong, H. "Buckwheat." *Field Crop Abstracts* 25 no. 3 (August 1972).

Eggum, Bjorn O. "The Protein Quality of Buckwheat in Comparison with Other Protein Sources of Plant or Animal Origin." In *Buckwheat Research 1980: Proceedings of the 1st International Symposium on Buckwheat.* Ljubljana, Yugoslavia: Organizing Committee of the 1st International Symposium on Buckwheat, 1980.

Eggum, Bjorn O., Ivan Kreft, and Branka, Javornik. "Chemical composition and protein quality of buckwheat (Fagopyrum esculentum moench)." Netherlands: Martinus Nijhoff/Dr. W. Junk, 1981.

Everett, Thomas H., ed. *The New York Botanical Garden Illustrated Encyclopedia of Horticulture.* Vol 4. New York and London: Garland Publishing, 1981.

Fujimura, Masao. *Soba no gijutsu* (Soba technique). Tokyo: Shokuhin Shuppansha, 1980.

Furuzawa, Norio. *Iwate no soba* (Soba of Iwate Prefecture). Morioka Japan: Kumagai Insatsu, 1985.

*Great Soviet Encyclopedia: A Translation of the Third Edition.* Vol. 7. New York: Macmillan; London: Collier Macmillan, 1972.

Hagami, Rev. Shocho. "Mt. Hiei and Buckwheat." In *Buckwheat Research 1983: Proceedings of the 2nd International Symposium on Buckwheat.* Ed. Takashi Nagamoto and Taiji Adachi. Miyazaki, Japan: Organizing Committee of the 2nd International Symposium on Buckwheat, 1983.

Harlan, Jack R. "Agricultural Origins: Center and Noncenters." *Science* 174 (October 1971).

Hunt, Thomas F. *The Cereals in America.* New York: Orange Judd Company; London: Kegan Paul, Trench, Trubner and Co., Ltd., 1914.

International Symposium on Buckwheat, Ljubljana, Yugoslavia, 1980. *Buckwheat Research 1980: Proceedings of the 1st International Symposium on Buckwheat.* Ljubljana, Yugoslavia: Organizing Committee of the 1st International Symposium on Buckwheat, 1980. See also under Eggum, Bjorn O.; Javornik, Branka, and Ivan Kreft; and Kreft, Ivan, and Branka Javornik.

International Symposium on Buckwheat, Miyazaki, Japan, 1983. *Buckwheat Research 1983: Proceedings of the 2nd International Symposium on Buckwheat.* Miyazaki Pref., Japan: Organizing Committee of the 2nd International Symposium on Buckwheat, 1983. See also under Hagami, Rev. Shocho; Kreft, Ivan; and Javornik, Branka.

Japan. Science and Technology Agency. *Standard Tables of Food Composition in Japan.* 4th ed. Tokyo: 1982.

Javornik, Branka. "Nutritional Quality and Composition of Buckwheat Proteins." In *Buckwheat Research 1983: Proceedings of the 2nd International Symposium on Buckwheat.* Ed. Takashi Nagamoto and Taiji Adachi. Miyazaki, Japan: Organizing Committee of the 2nd International Symposium on Buckwheat, 1983.

Javornik, Branka, and Ivan Kreft. "The Structure of the Buckwheat Kernel." In *Buckwheat Research 1980: Proceedings of the 1st International Symposium on Buckwheat.* Ljubljana, Yugoslavia: Organizing Committee of the 1st International Symposium on Buckwheat, 1980.

Kaneko, Manpei. *Shinshu soba no hanashi* (Shinshu soba wisdom). 1975. Reprint Japan: Shinshu Ginga Shobo, 1979.

Kreft, Ivan. "Buckwheat Breeding Perspectives." In *Buckwheat Research 1983: Proceedings of the 2nd International Symposium on Buckwheat.* Ed. Takashi Nagamoto and Taiji Adachi. Miyazaki, Japan: Organizing Committee of the 2nd International Symposium on Buckwheat, 1983.

Kreft, Ivan, and Branka Javornik. "Traditional

Processing and Utilization of Buckwheat in Yugoslavia." In *Buckwheat Research 1980: Proceedings of the 1st International Symposium on Buckwheat*. Ljubljana, Yugoslavia: Organizing Committee of the 1st International Symposium on Buckwheat, 1980.

Muramoto, Noboru. *Healing Ourselves*. Avon, N.Y.: Avon Press, 1972.

Nasu, Keisuke. *Kenko soba* (Healthful soba). Tokyo: Nosan Gyoson Bunka Kyokai, 1984.

Niijima, Shigeru. *Soba nyumon* (An introduction to soba). Tokyo: Hoiku-sha, 1975.

Niijima, Shigeru, and Shigehisa Shibata. *Menrui hyakka jiten* (Encyclopedia of noodles). Tokyo: Shokuhin Shuppan-sha, 1984.

Nishio, Yoshihiro. "Hinoemata no soba ryori" (Soba cooking of Hinoemata [home of the "silk cut" soba]). In *Tohoku II*, Vol. 2 of *Nihon no kyodo ryori* (Japanese country cooking). Tokyo: Gyosei, 1986.

Ohsawa, George. *The Philosophy of Oriental Medicine*. Vol. 2, *The Book of Judgment*. 1960. 2d ed. published as *The Book of Judgment*. New York: Ohsawa Foundation, 1966.

Ohsawa, George. *Zen Cookery: The Philosophy of Oriental Culture*. Vol. 1, *Practical Macrobiotics*. 1963. Reprint. Los Angeles: Ignoramus Press, 1966.

*The Oxford English Dictionary—A New English Dictionary on Historical Principles*. London: Oxford, 1933.

Sekai Bunka Sha. *Furusato soba udon* (Country-style soba and udon). Tokyo, 1984.

———. *Soba*. In *Oishii men* (Delicious noodles). Tokyo, 1983.

Sherry, Robert W. *Plants for Man*. 2d ed. Englewood Cliffs, N.J.: Prentice-Hall Inc., 1972.

Shibata Shoten. *Masshiro ni saita soba: soba mukashi banashi* (The white blossoming soba: Tales of soba). Tokyo, 1984.

———. *Soba udon gijutsu kyohon* (A manual of soba and udon technique). Vol. 1, *Soba no kihon gijutsu* (Basic soba technique). Tokyo, 1983. Vol. 2, *Soba udon no oyo gijutsu* (Advanced techniques of soba and udon). Tokyo, 1985.

———. *Soba udon: New Menu*. Tokyo, 1986.

Shurtleff, William, and Akiko Aoyagi *The Book of Tofu*. 1973. Reprint. Berkeley: Ten Speed Press, 1983.

Takase, Reibun. *Soba no hon* (The book of soba). Tokyo: Bunka Shuppan Kyoku, 1983.

Tsuchiya, Yoshio. *A Feast for the Eyes: The Japanese Art of Food Arrangement*. Tokyo and New York: Kodansha International, 1985.

Tsuji, Keisuke. *Shitekiso shoku no kenko ho* (The healthy way of balanced eating). Tokyo: Kobunsha, 1983.

———. "Soba no eiyo" (The multi-working nutritional power of buckwheat). *Soba udon* 14 (June 1984).

Tsuji, Shizuo. *Japanese Cooking: A Simple Art*. Tokyo and New York: Kodansha International, 1980.

Tsuji, Shizuo, and Koichiro Hata. *Practical Japanese Cooking: Easy and Elegant*. Tokyo and New York: Kodansha International, 1986.

Uehara, Jiro, and Ryuichi Satsuma. *Soba no hon* (The book of soba). Tokyo: Shibata Shoten, 1969.

Uji, Masami. "Soba yo sake yo te o tsunage" (Soba and saké join hands). In *Soba shikomi-cho seken-banashi* (Soba preparation and discussion). Nagano, Japan: Ginga Shobo, 1987.

Ujihara, Akio. *Soba no kagaku: Nihon soba no ruutsu to soba no shokumotsushi* (The roots and history of buckwheat as a foodstuff). Tokyo: Mainichi Shinbunsha Shuppan, 1981.

———. "Studies on the ecological features and the potentials as breeding materials of Asian common buckwheat varieties (Fagopyrum esculentum M.)." Tokyo: Ministry of Education and Ministry of Agriculture, Forestry and Fisheries, 1983.

Vavilov, N. I. *The Origin, Variation, Immunity and Breeding of Cultivated Plants* (in Russian). 1934. Translated by K. Starr Chester in *Selected Writings of N. I. Vavilov*. Waltham, Mass.: Chronica Botanica, 1950.

Yoneda, Soei. *The Heart of Zen Cuisine*. Originally published as *Good Food from a Japanese Temple*. 1982. Tokyo and New York: Kodansha International, 1987.

# Index

# Acknowledgments

I wish to express my gratitude to all those who have given me support, assistance, and advice on this project and over the years:

To my three soba teachers, Takao Abe of Take Yabu, Shigeru Fujimori of Fujisei, and Ikuma Yamamoto of Honjinbo for allowing me to work and train within the confines of their traditional shops, thereby giving me the chance to study the art backstage. Their perseverance and pride inspired me to take the job seriously.

To the soba masters of Honmura-an, Wakatake, Shungetsu, and Okina for welcoming me into their establishments and teaching me the secrets of home milling, emphasizing that quality home grinding can be done successfully. To Yoshiyuki Oyama of Honjinbo and Fumio Hirai of Take Yabu for their assistance in preparing the menu for the color photographs. To Tae Moriyama, Tami Ejima, Hideo Sakai, Chiyako Hatsuyama, Chika Furukawa, and many others whose help was indispensable in helping me meet the formidable challenge of reading vital Japanese texts.

To William and Akiko Shurtleff, who, in addition to providing a wealth of specific research contributions which added immeasurable depth to my own understanding of soba and its history in the West, have been trusty consultants on how to introduce soba to the West. To Yuichi Nagata for providing me with a variety of written material on soba in Japanese and for kindly introducing me to the soba historian Shigeru Niijima, and Professor and Mrs. Akio Ujihara of Shinshu University. Hosting me on three separate occasions, Ujihara's broad knowledge and understanding of soba greatly enlarged my own vision. To Yachiyo ("As in the Japanese national anthem") and Yoshinaka Hirano of the "Corner store" (Kadoya) in Hinoemata, Fukushima Prefecture, for their kindness and assistance in the teaching and demonstration of the "Silk Cut" method and other country originals, and to Morikatsu Hirano for demonstrating the traditional kibachi-making method. To Satsuma Uichi, president of the highly respected Mimi-yu restaurant, for showing me the workings of his restaurant in Kyobashi, where, in addition to maintaining a unique expertise in udon noodle making, they take pride in creating fine soba. To Dr. Bjorn Eggum and Professor Ivan Kreft for supplying important scientific data in time to reach the publication deadline, and to Dr. Keisuke Tsuji, who spent three afternoons making sure I understood his nutrition report, as well as correcting mistakes in the final draft.

To my brothers Drs. Robert and Richard Udesky, for their encouragement in the promotion of a food that is "low in fat and cholesterol free." To my sister, Joan, who knew from the start that I was up to something more than just making noodles and has been faithfully keeping me up-to-date on developments in the Natural Food movement back home. To the friends and colleagues who, over the last fifteen years, have helped me, directly and indirectly, in the writing of this book: Mark Gray who was with me throughout the eight years of training and writing in Japan; Bob and Martha Newmiller; Elliott Lash; Jacob Israel; and Dr. Richard Harris, who introduced me to the way of Natural Food in America. To Noboru Muramoto, and Herman and Cornellia Aihara for initially sending me to Japan in 1977, and whose guidance and fundamental teachings from 1972 to 1976 continue to serve me tremendously.

To Ryuji Koseta of the Federation of Japan Noodle Organizations, representing more than 20,000 soba shops in Japan, for his untiring assistance and dedication to the promotion of soba. Special thanks go to Hitoshi Matsuura of the Japan Victor Company and Shigeo Sugawa and Tatsu Yasuhara of Dentsu for their encouragement, guidance, and unselfish support, spurring me on until the end. To Kenzaburo Mogi and Linda Sakamoto of the Kikkoman Corporation for their generosity and interest in this project. To Yasuo and Koji Ishimori of the Ishimori Buckwheat Milling Company for extending their cooperation and hospitality on many occasions.

Finally, thanks are in order to the people at Kodansha International: Koki Mori for his expert counsel; Barry Lancet for his fine editing and for first suggesting I bring my manuscript to KI; Makiko Sasaki for her editorial work; Shigeo Katakura for his design; Kensuke Tada, Prue Moodie, and Michiko Tsukamoto for help in the final hour; and lastly, to Keiji Suzuki, whose love of soba rivals my own, and whose encouragement continues to give me hope that buckwheat will finally receive its due attention in the West, and once again demonstrate its true status as a food of the people.

For further information on soba write to
**The Soba Center**
P.O. Box 72
Winnetka, ILL 60093-0072

Cooperation and invaluable assistance in the production of this book were given by the following soba shops, companies, and associations: Honjinbo, Take Yabu, Fujisei, Asanoya, Honmura-an. Kikkoman, Ozeki, Ishimori Seifun-jo, Odakyu Department Store (in Shinjuku), Seibu Department Store (in Ikebukuro), Matsuya Department Store (in Ginza), Nushisa Shikki-ten. Federation of Japan Noodle Organizations, Japan Buckwheat Millers Association.

CREDITS
Photography by Tamihisa Ejiri. Additional photographs: Tetsu Hayakawa, pp. 14, 17–28, 51 (top); Federation of Japan Noodle Organizations, pp. 4, 13; Dr. Akio Ujihara, pp. 46 (bottom), 47 (top right); Kodansha Photo Library, pp. 46 (top), 47 (top left), 52 (top, bottom left). *Ukiyo-e* and *Nihonga* prints courtesy of Jyutaro Yamamoto. Sketches in recipe sections by Reiko Michida. Sketches in appendices by Ryosuke Kami.

撮影並びにご指導、ご協力いただきました各位には、
厚く御礼申し上げます。

_____

〈そば店〉

本陣房　　　　東京都港区西新橋1-5-10

竹やぶ　　　　千葉県柏市柏1144-2

藤盛　　　　　東京都杉並区西荻北3-19-13

かどや　　　　福島県南会津郡桧枝岐村

浅野屋　　　　東京都文京区水道2-5-8

本むら庵　　　東京都杉並区上荻2-7-11

〈その他〉

キッコーマン株式会社海外事業部
　　　　　　　　　東京都千代田区神田錦町1-25

大関株式会社　西宮市今津出在家町四番九号

石森製粉所　　東京都中野区本町1-32-27

ぬしさ漆器　　東京都台東区東上野2-10-12

松屋　　　　　東京都中央区銀座3-6-1

小田急百貨店　東京都新宿区西新宿1-1-3

西武百貨店　　東京都豊島区南池袋1-28-1

日本麺類業団体連合会　東京都千代田区神田神保町2-4

全国蕎麦製粉共同組合　東京都豊島区駒込1-40-4

氏原暉男農学博士　信州大学農学部作物・育種学研究室
　　　　　　　　　長野県上伊那郡南箕輪村8304

〈蕎麦浮世絵提供〉

山本重太郎

定価2,200円